Integrated Chinese

CHENG & TSUI PUBLICATIONS OF RELATED INTEREST

Making Connections: Enhance Your Listening Comprehension in Chinese (Text & Audio CD Set)
Madeline K. Spring

▲ Includes lessons for *Integrated Chinese* users.

Simplified Characters   0-88727-366-1
Traditional Characters   0-88727-365-3

Chinese BuilderCards: The Lightning Path to Mastering Vocabulary
Song Jiang and Haidan Wang

▲ Includes vocabulary from *Integrated Chinese*.

Simplified Characters   0-88727-434-X
Traditional Characters   0-88727-426-9

Cheng & Tsui Chinese-Pinyin-English Dictionary for Learners
Wang Huan, Editor-in-Chief

Paperback   0-88727-316-5

Cheng & Tsui Chinese Character Dictionary
Wang Huidi, Editor-in-Chief

Paperback   0-88727-314-9

**Crossing Paths: Living and Learning in China,
An Intermediate Chinese Course**
Hong Gang Jin and De Bao Xu, with Der-lin Chao, Yea-fen Chen, and Min Chen

Paperback & Audio CD Set   0-88727-370-X

**Success with Chinese: A Communicative Approach for Beginners,
Reading & Writing Book**
De-an Wu Swihart

Paperback   0-88727-475-7

Pop Chinese: A Cheng & Tsui Handbook of Contemporary Colloquial Expressions
Yu Feng, Yaohua Shi, Zhijie Jia, Judith M. Amory, and Jie Cai

Paperback   0-88727-424-2

Please visit **www.cheng-tsui.com** for more information on these and many other language-learning resources, or visit **www.webtech.cheng-tsui.com** for information on web-based and downloadable products.

Integrated Chinese

中文聽說讀寫

Traditional and Simplified Character Edition

CHARACTER WORKBOOK

2nd Edition

Tao-chung Yao and Yuehua Liu

**Jeffrey J. Hayden, Xiaojun Wang, Yea-fen Chen,
Liangyan Ge, Nyan-ping Bi & Yaohua Shi**

CHENG & TSUI COMPANY ▲ Boston

10 09 08 07 06   10 9 8 7 6 5 4 3

Published by
Cheng & Tsui Company
25 West Street
Boston, MA 02111-1213 USA
Fax (617) 426-3669
www.cheng-tsui.com
"Bringing Asia to the World"™

Printed in the U.S.A.

ISBN 0-88727-438-2

The *Integrated Chinese* series includes books, workbooks, character workbooks, audio products, multimedia products, teacher's resources, and more. Visit **www.cheng-tsui.com** for more information on the other components of *Integrated Chinese*.

THE INTEGRATED CHINESE SERIES

The *Integrated Chinese* series is a two-year course that includes textbooks, workbooks, character workbooks, audio CDs, CD-ROMs, DVDs, and teacher's resources.

Textbooks introduce Chinese language and culture through a series of dialogues and narratives, with culture notes, language use and grammar explanations, and exercises.

Workbooks follow the format of the textbooks and contain a wide range of integrated activities that teach the four language skills of listening, speaking, reading, and writing.

Character Workbooks help students learn Chinese characters in their correct stroke order. Special emphasis is placed on the radicals that are frequently used to compose Chinese characters.

Audio CDs include the narratives, dialogues and vocabulary presented in the textbooks, as well as pronunciation and listening exercises that correspond to the workbooks.

Teacher's Resources contain answer keys, transcripts of listening exercises, grammar notes, and helpful guidance on using the series in the classroom.

Multimedia CD-ROMs are divided into sections of listening, speaking, reading, and writing, and feature a variety of supplemental interactive games and activities for students to test their skills and get instant feedback.

In the **Workbook DVD,** the dialogues from the Level 1 Part 1 Workbook are presented in contemporary settings in color video format.

PUBLISHER'S NOTE

When *Integrated Chinese* was first published in 1997, it set a new standard with its focus on the development and integration of the four language skills (listening, speaking, reading, and writing). Today, to further enrich the learning experience of the many users of *Integrated Chinese* worldwide, the Cheng & Tsui Company is pleased to offer the revised, updated and expanded second edition of *Integrated Chinese*. We would like to thank the many teachers and students who, by offering their valuable insights and suggestions, have helped *Integrated Chinese* evolve and keep pace with the many positive changes in the field of Chinese language instruction. *Integrated Chinese* continues to offer comprehensive language instruction, with many new features.

The Cheng & Tsui Asian Language Series is designed to publish and widely distribute quality language learning materials created by leading instructors from around the world. We welcome readers' comments and suggestions concerning the publications in this series. Please send feedback to our Editorial Department (e-mail: **editor@cheng-tsui.com**), or contact the following members of our Editorial Board.

Professor Shou-hsin Teng, *Chief Editor*
3 Coach Lane, Amherst, MA 01002

Professor Dana Scott Bourgerie
Asian and Near Eastern Languages
Brigham Young University, Provo, UT 84602

Professor Samuel Cheung
Dept. of Chinese, Chinese University of Hong Kong,
Shatin, Hong Kong

Professor Ying-che Li
Dept. of East Asian Languages, University of Hawaii,
Honolulu, HI 96822

Professor Timothy Light
Dept. of Comparative Religion, Western Michigan University,
Kalamazoo, MI 49008

CONTENTS

Lessons

Indexes

PREFACE

This Character Workbook is a companion volume to *Integrated Chinese* Textbook, Level 1, Part 1. The *Integrated Chinese* series is an acclaimed, best-selling introductory course in Mandarin Chinese. With its holistic, integrated focus on the four language skills of listening, speaking, reading, and writing, it teaches all the basics beginning and intermediate students need to function in Chinese. *Integrated Chinese* helps students understand how the Chinese language works grammatically, and how to use Chinese in real life.

This book is designed to help students learn Chinese characters in their correct stroke order, and then by their components. We believe that the student will learn a new character more easily if s/he can identify the components in each character and know why the specific components are used in each character. Therefore we strongly urge teachers to teach their students the 40 basic radicals, which are frequently used to compose Chinese characters.

The Importance of Learning Radicals

When learning a new character, the first thing that the student should do is to try to identify the known component(s). By doing that, the student will only need to remember what components are in the character, rather than remember the composition of many meaningless strokes. For example, both 女 (nǔ, *female*) and 馬 (mǎ, *horse*) are taught in the radical section. When the student sees the character 媽 (mā, *mother*) in Lesson 2, s/he should be able to tell that the new character 媽 consists of two known components, namely, 女 and 馬. The components in a character sometimes give clues to the meaning and pronunciation of the character. The radical 女 in the character 媽 suggests that the character might be related to females, and the other component, 馬, is a phonetic element giving a clue to its pronunciation. If a student can remember that the character for "mother" sounds like "horse," he/she would have an easier time learning how to write the character. It would be a very painful way to learn the character 媽 if all one sees is a character consisting of a number of meaningless strokes, with a few vertical lines, a few horizontal lines, and a few dots.

The 40 radicals selected here, of course, are just some of the components that are seen in Chinese characters. However, by mastering these 40 radicals, the student will realize that many characters contain one or two of the 40 components, and that the student only needs to concentrate on the new components that s/he has not seen before. By knowing the meanings and the pronunciations of the components of the new character, the student will be able to retain the shape and the sound of the new character better.

Numbers

After the "Radicals" section in this workbook, there is a small section on numerals. Since numbers are extremely useful in everyday life, we urge students to learn the characters 1–10 as soon as possible. Also, these characters are quite easy to write and can serve as a good introductory lesson for beginning students.

How This Book Is Designed

Each page of this Character Workbook has four to five new characters on it. Each new character is displayed in a large point size on the left side of the page, with the traditional (complex) form on the left and the simplified form on the right. The *pīnyīn* reading and English translation are immediately to the right of these. An asterisk (*) before an English translation means that the character is bound to another character and that the English translation represents the meaning of the compound rather than the individual character. Next to the *pīnyīn* reading there is a number in parentheses, which represents the ranking of the character given in the *Xiàndài Hànyǔ Pínlù Cídiǎn* (《现代汉语频率词典》, *The Dictionary of Modern Chinese Word Frequency*). For example, for the character 人 (rén, *person*), the number "9" given in the parentheses means that this character is the ninth most frequently used character in the Chinese written language. The symbol "†" in the parentheses indicates that the character does not belong to the 1000 most frequently used characters according to the *Xiàndài Hànyǔ Pínlù Cídiǎn*. While we try to introduce the first 1000 most frequently used characters in the first two levels of *Integrated Chinese*, we sometimes have to include some characters beyond the first thousand to make the text natural and functional.

In the "Radicals" section, under the English translation of the character, the same radical is found in a smaller size. If the radical has a variation, then the variation is given to the right of the smaller character. If the radical has a simplified version, this is given in the third square. There are only three radicals that have stand-alone simplified characters.

In the main lessons, both traditional and simplified characters are provided together. Both forms will have the strokes numbered. Immediately to the right of the large character(s), underneath the *pīnyīn* and English definition, are smaller versions of the character(s). The first will show the radical of the character in black, with the rest of the character in gray. When a simplified version of the character exists, it is given to the right of the smaller traditional character. If a variant of the character exists, it will be provided in the third square and will have the small symbol "Δ" after it indicating the "printing/variant form." Students should learn how to write the "written form," i.e., the large character.

Each practicing unit for a character contains three or four rows of small boxes. The first row to the right of the *pīnyīn* and English has two grayed characters. The student is expected to trace these. If the character has a simplified form, this will appear underneath the grayed traditional characters. The final three boxes at the end of the first and second rows are in graph-style layout to facilitate practice of character proportion. The remaining row(s) have at their head (the far left) small versions of the character (traditional, and, where one exists, simplified). To the right of these the characters have been penned in according to their proper stroke orders. The remaining empty boxes are for the student to practice writing the character in free form. By this time in the process, the student should be expected to be able to draw the character in proper spatial proportions without the use of any guides.

It is very important that each character is drawn in the correct stroke order. Two devices are used in this workbook to show a character's stroke order. The small numbers printed along the large characters indicate the sequence of the strokes. In general, every effort has been made to place the number at the starting point of the stroke. Because in some instances it is not very easy to tell which number goes with what stroke, or to tell where each stroke begins and ends, a "pen version" of each character is provided. Immediately below the large character, the character is drawn one step at a time to show how it is formed. Students should consult this series of strokes when practicing writing characters.

For components that have previously appeared, the pen version may simply show the entire component already drawn rather than writing it out one stroke at a time. For example, the pen version for the character 明 (míng, *bright*) in Lesson 4 uses only two boxes, one for 日, and one for 明. This means that when writing the character 明, one first writes 日, and then one writes 月 next to 日 to form 明. No individual strokes are given here because the student has already learned how to write 日 and 月 separately.

Additional Resources

There are many computer programs (such as *Chinese Character Tutor* by Ted Yao and Mark Peterson and *Hanzi Assistant* by Panda Software) that are designed to teach stroke order. Students are encouraged to use them if they have access to the software. For more information on computer software for learning Chinese characters, and to share ideas with other users of the *Integrated Chinese* series, please visit http://EALL.hawaii.edu/yao/ICUsers/. Jeffrey J. Hayden has also created printable flash cards covering all the characters introduced in this textbook. These and many other materials related to *Integrated Chinese* may be found at http://www2.hawaii.edu/~jeffrey/.

To learn more about the *Integrated Chinese* series, get the latest product updates, and find other supplementary resources, please visit the official *Integrated Chinese* website by going to **http://www.cheng-tsui.com/contact.asp**, and clicking on the link for the *Integrated Chinese* website.

About This New Edition

The three people who have spent the most time in preparing this version of the *Integrated Chinese* Level 1 Part 1 Character Workbook are Jeffrey J. Hayden, Xiaojun Wang, and Ted Tao-chung Yao. Based on suggestions provided by teachers at the Chinese Language Instructional Materials (CLIM) conference held in Honolulu in July 2003, Hayden incorporated his design model for the *Integrated Chinese* Level 2 Character Workbook into this combined traditional/simplified edition, which includes material previously designed for the separate traditional and simplified editions of the *Integrated Chinese* Level 1 Character Workbooks. Wang has again done the pen version stroke ordering in this edition.

人		rén (9) man; person		人	人		
		人	亻				
人	ノ	人					
亻	ノ	亻					

刀		dāo (789) knife		刀	刀		
		刀	刂				
刀	フ	刀					
刂	丨	刂					

力		lì (119) power		力	力		
		力					
力	フ	力					

又		yòu (65) right hand; again		又	又		
		又					
又	フ	又					

口		kǒu (182) mouth		口	口		
		口					
口	丨	冂	口				

		wéi (†)		口	口			
口		enclose						
			口		人			
口	丨	冂	口					

**Used as a radical only, not as a character by itself.

		tǔ (373)		土	土			
土		earth						
			土					
土	一	十	土					

		xī (†)		夕	夕			
夕		sunset						
			夕					
夕	丿	勺	夕					

		dà (17)		大	大			
大		big; large						
			大					
大	一	ナ	大					

		nǚ (299)		女	女			
女		female; woman						
			女					
女	く	乆	女					

子		zǐ (24) son	子	子			
		子					
子 ㇆ 了 子							

寸		cùn (†) inch	寸	寸			
		寸					
寸 一 寸 寸							

小		xiǎo (50) little; small; young	小	小			
		小					
小 亅 小 小							

工		gōng (55) labor; work	工	工			
		工					
工 一 丁 工							

幺		yāo (†) tiny; small	幺	幺			
		幺					
幺 乙 幺 幺							

弓		gōng (†) bow		弓	弓			
		弓						
弓	⁷	ㄢ	弓					

心		xīn (82) heart		心	心			
		心	忄					
心	⟍	心	心	心				
忄	⟍	忄	忄					

戈		gē (†) dagger-axe		戈	戈			
		戈						
戈	一	弋	戈	戈				

手		shǒu (115) hand		手	手			
		手	扌					
手	⟍	二	三	手				
扌	一	十	扌					

日		rì (269) sun		日	日			
		日						
日	丨	冂	日	日				

月		yuè　　　(207)	月	月			
		moon					
		月					
月	丿	刀	月	月			

木		mù　　　(607)	木	木			
		wood					
		木					
木	一	十	才	木			

水		shuǐ　　　(102)	水	水			
		water					
		水	氵				
水	丿	刀	才	水			
氵	丶	冫	氵				

火		huǒ　　　(308)	火	火			
		fire					
		火	灬				
火	丶	丷	少	火			
灬	丶	八	八	灬			

田		tián　　　(727)	田	田			
		field					
		田					
田	丨	冂	日	田	田		

目		mù (408)	目	目			
		eye					
		目					
目	丨	冂	冃	月	目		

示		shì (†)	示	示			
		to show					
		示	礻				
示	一	二	亍	亓	示		
礻	丶	丆	礻	礻			

糸		**mì (†)	糸	糸			
		fine silk					
		糸	糸	纟			
糸	乚	幺	幺	纟	糸	糸	
糸	乚	幺	幺	纟	糸	糸	
纟	乚	幺	纟				

**Used as a radical only, not as a character by itself.

耳		ěr (960)	耳	耳			
		ear					
		耳					
耳	一	丅	丁丁	丌	耳	耳	

衣		yī (473) clothing	衣 衣		
		衣 衤			
衣	丶	一	亠	衣	衣	衣
衤	丶	亠	礻	衤	礻

言		yán (655) speech	言 言		
		言 讠			
言	丶	二	亖	言	言	言
讠	丶	讠

貝 贝		bèi (†) cowry (shell)	貝 貝		
		貝 贝	贝 贝		
貝	丨	冂	冃	月	目	貝	貝
贝	丨	冂	刀	贝

走		zǒu (104) to walk	走 走		
		走			
走	一	十	土	士	卡	赤	走

足		zú (758)	足	足				
		foot						
		足	疋					
足	丶	丨丶	口	묘	무	尹	足	
疋	丶	口	口	묘	무	尹	足	

金		jīn (514)	金	金				
		metal; gold						
		金	釒	钅				
金	丿	人	亼	今	仐	㑒	釡	金
釒	丿	人	亼	仝	仐	今	釡	釒
钅	丿	人	仁	仨	钅			

門	门	mén (199)	門	門				
		door						
		門		门	门	门		
門	丨	尸	尸	尸	冃	門	門	門
门	丶	冫	门					

隹		zhuī (†)	隹	隹				
		short-tailed bird						
		隹						
隹	丿	亻	亻	仁	仨	隹	隹	隹

雨		yǔ (542) rain		雨	雨			
		雨	雷					
雨	一	厂	冂	吊	雨	雨	雨	雨
雷	一	冖	冖	雫	雫	雫	雷	雷

食		shí (549) to eat		食	食			
		食	食	仓				
食	丿	人	𠆢	今	今	令	食	食	食
食	丿	𠆢	𠆢	今	今	令	食	食
仓	丿	𠆢	仑					

馬 马		mǎ (359) horse		馬	馬			
		馬	马	马	马			
馬	一	厂	𠃌	𠃌	馬	馬	馬	馬	馬
马	𠃌	马	马					

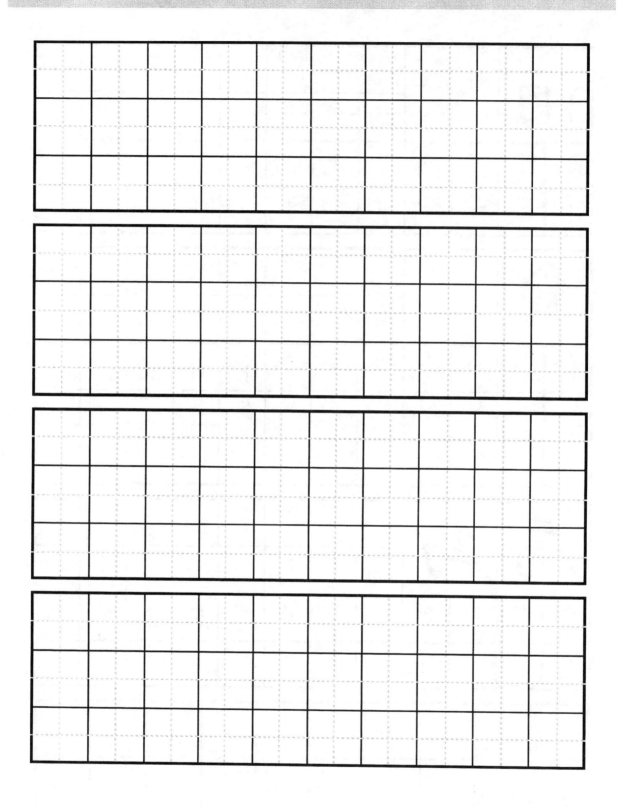

一		yī (2) one						
		一						
一	一							

二		èr (118) two						
		二						
二	二							

三		sān (106) three						
		三						
三	一	二	三					

四		sì (166) four	四	四				
		四	四	四	四	四		
四	丨	冂	四	四	四			

五		wǔ (195) five	五	五				
		五	五	五	五	五		
五	一	丁	五	五	五	五	五	

六		liù　　　(358) six	六 六				
		六 六					
六	丶	亠	亣	六			

七		qī　　　(393) seven	七 七				
		七					
七	一	七					

八		bā　　　(323) eight	八 八				
		八					
八	丿	八					

九		jiǔ　　　(264) nine	九 九				
		九 九					
九	丿	九					

十		shí　　　(79) ten	十 十				
		十					
十	一	十					

Dialogue I

先		xiān (179) first	先 先			
		先 先 先 先 先				
先	ノ	⺊	生	牛	先 先 先 先 先 先

生		shēng (42) to be born	生 生			
		生 生 生 生 生 生 生 生				
生	ノ	⺊	仁	牛	生 生 生 生 生 生 生

你		nǐ (20) you	你 你			
		你 你 你 你 你				
你	亻	亻	伈	你 你 你 你 你 你 你 你

好		hǎo / hào (40) fine; good; OK	好 好			
		好 好 好 好 好 好				
好	女	好	好	好	好

小		xiǎo (50) little; small; young	小 小			
		小 小 小 小 小				
小	小			小 小 小 小 小

姐		jiě (693) older sister	姐	姐			
		姐 姐 姐					
姐	女	刘	如	姐	姐	姐	

王		wáng (863) (a surname); king	王	王			
		王					
王	一	二	干	王			

李		lǐ (†) (a surname); plum	李	李			
		李					
李	木	李					

| 請 请 | qǐng (547) please; to invite | 請 请 | | 請 请 | 請 请 | | |
| 請 请 | 言 讠 | 言 讠 | 訂 订 | 訃 讠 | 詿 讠 | 請 请 | |

請   請   請

問	问	wèn　　　(112) to ask	問	问

問	門	問
问	门	问

您		nín　　　(237) you (polite)　您

您	你	您

貴	贵	guì　　　(†) honorable; expensive	貴	贵	貴

貴	口	中	虫	貴	貴	貴	貴
贵	口	中	虫	贵			

姓		xìng　　　(†) surname　姓

姓	女	姓

我		wǒ (6)	我	我			
		I; me					
		我					
我	丶	二	千	手	扎	我	我

呢		ne (151)	呢	呢			
		QP					
		呢					
呢	口	口フ	口コ	叺	叺	呢	

叫		jiào (154)	叫	叫			
		to be called					
		叫					
叫	口	叮	叫				

什		shén (80)	什	什			
		*what					
		什		甚 △			
什	亻	什					

(Note: The simplified form is taught here because the traditional form is rarely used now.)

麼么		me (27) *QP	麼 麼			
麼	`	亠 广 床 麻 麼 麼 麼 麼				
么	ノ 厶					

| 名 | | míng name 名 | 名 名 | | | |
| 名 夕 名 | | | | | | |

| 字 | | zì character 字 | 字 字 | | | |
| 字 ` ` 宀 字 | | | | | | |

| 朋 | | péng friend 朋 | 朋 朋 | | | |
| 朋 月 朋 | | | | | | |

| 友 | | yǒu friend 友 | 友 友 | | | |
| 友 一 ナ 友 | | | | | | |

see page 141

Dialogue II

是		shì (4) to be	是	是			
		是					

是	日	旦	早	昆	是	是	

老		lǎo (87) old	老	老			
		老					

老	土	少	老				

師	师	shī (310) teacher	師	師			
		師	师	師	师		

師	′	⺅	⼾	戶	㠯	自	𠂤	師	師	師
师	′	⼅	广	师	师	师				

嗎	吗	ma (248) QP	嗎	嗎			
		嗎	吗	吗	吗		

嗎	口	嗎					
吗	口	吗					

嗎　　　嗎　　　嗎

| | | bù (5)
not; no | 不 | 不 | | | |
|不| | 不 | | | | | |

不 一 丆 不 不

		xué (46) to study	學	學			
學 學		學 學 學	學 學			
see page 141						

學 ` ⺈ ⺊ ⺊ ⺊ ⺊ 臼 臼 臼 臼 臼

臼 學

学 ` ⸌ ⸌ ⸌ ⸌ 学

| | | yě (30)
too; also | 也 | 也 | | | |
|也| | 也 | | | | | |

也 ⺄ 乜 也

| | | zhōng (61)
center; middle | 中 | 中 | | | |
|中| | 中 | | | | | |

中 中

學 學 學

國	国	guó (37) country			國	国			
		國	国	國	國	国			
國	门	門	冋	冋	國	國	國	國	
国	冂	囯	国	国	國	國	國		

人		rén (9) person; people			人	人			
		人							
人	丿	人							

美		měi (593) beautiful		美	美				
		美							
美	丶	ʾ	丷	兰	羊	羊	美		

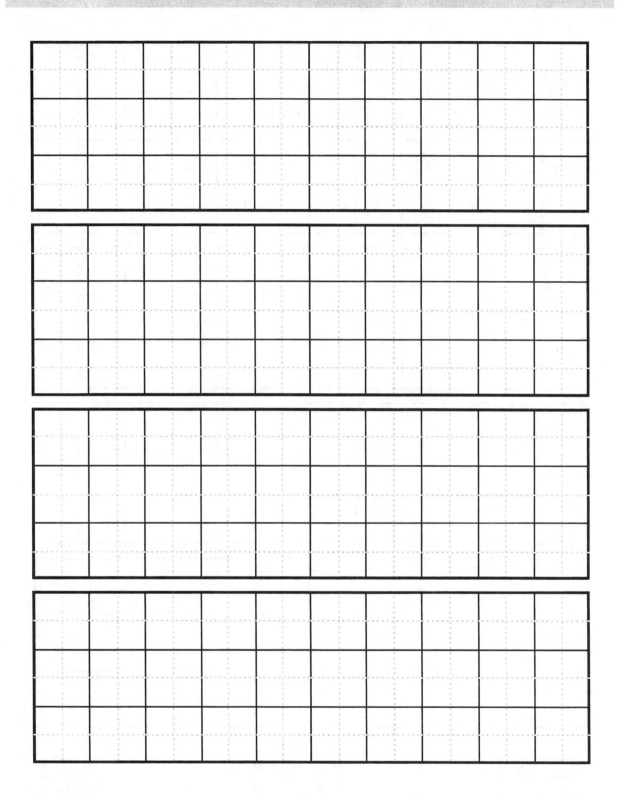

Fun With Characters

I. SEEK AND FIND.

Hidden in the box below are some phrases from the text. See how many you can find and circle them. Phrases can go horizontally left to right (→), vertically top to bottom (↓), or diagonally upper left to lower right (↘) or lower left to upper right (↗).

我	是	學	生	你	呢	你
我	不	李	你	人	朋	叫
也	姓	是	美	是	友	什
你	好	王	老	師	誰	麼
姓	中	貴	國	師	人	名
李	小	姐	你	好	嗎	字
嗎	你	是	學	生	嗎	誰

II. RADICAL IDENTIFICATION.

Provide the Pīnyīn for each of the following characters and put the radical component each set has in common in the parentheses to the right. [Hint: Refer to the Radicals section (pp. 1-10).]

你 _____   什 _____   (_____)

好 _____   姐 _____   姓 _____   (_____)

呢 _____   叫 _____   嗎 (吗) _____   (_____)

好 _____   李 _____   學 (学) _____   (_____)

III. MATCHING.

First, draw a line connecting the Pīnyīn to its traditional character. Then, connect the traditional character to its simplified counterpart. Finally, draw a line connecting the simplified character to its English meaning.

Pīnyīn	Traditional	Simplified	English
guì	師	学	QP
guó	請	么	to ask
ma	嗎	贵	to study
me	問	问	honorable
qǐng	學	国	teacher
shī	貴	师	to invite
wèn	國	吗	*QP
xué	麼	请	country

IV. PHONETIC IDENTIFICATION.

Provide the Pīnyīn for each of the following characters and provide the "phonetic" ("sound radical/component") in the parentheses along with its Pīnyīn. [Hint: Refer to the Radicals section (pp. 1-10).] The first two have been done for you.

姐   __jiě__   (__且__   __qiě__)

麼 (么) __me__   (__麻__   __má__)

問 (问) _____   (_____   _____)

嗎 (吗) _____   (_____   _____)

字 _____   (_____   _____)

友 _____   (_____   _____)

您 _____   (_____   _____)

Dialogue I

那	那	nà / nèi (31) that	那	那			
		那 那	那	那			
那	フ	フ	彐	尹	邪	邪	那
那	フ	フ	彐	尹	邪	那	

張	张	zhāng (431) M; (a surname)	張	張			
		張 张 張	張	張			
張	弓	弘	弘	驴	驴	弡	張	張	張
张	弓	弓	弘	张	张		

照		zhào (388) to shine	照	照			
		照					
照	日	旫	昭	照			

片		piàn / piān (413) *film; slice	片	片			
		片					
片	ノ	丿	广	片			

張 張 張

| 的 | | de / dí   (1) P | 的 | 白 | | 的 | 的 | | | |
| 的 | ㇔ | 白 | 白 | 的 | 的 | | | | | |

這 这		zhè / zhèi (10) this	這	这		這	這			
						这	这			
這	言	言	诘	诘	這					
这	㇔	亠	文	文	这	这				

| 爸 | | bà   (390) dad | 爸 | | | 爸 | 爸 | | | |
| 爸 | ㇒ | 八 | 父 | 父 | 谷 | 谷 | 爸 | 爸 | | |

媽 妈		mā (180) mom	媽	妈		媽	媽			
						妈	妈			
媽	女	媽								
妈	女	妈								

這　　　這　　　這

個	个	gè (14) M (general)				個	個		
		個	个	個	个	个			
個	亻	们	們	個	個	個	個		
个	人	个							

男		nán (937) male		男	男		
		男		男			
男	田	男					

孩		hái (304) child		孩	孩		
		孩		孩	孩	孩	
孩	子	孑	孓	孒	孩	孩	

子		zǐ (24) son; child		子	子		
		子					
子	了	子					

孩   孩   孩

誰	谁	shéi (353)	誰	谁			
		QPr; who?					
		誰	谁		誰	谁	
誰	言	誰					
谁	讠	谁					

他		tā (11)	他	他			
		he; him					
		他					
他	亻	他					

弟		dì (431)	弟	弟			
		younger brother					
		弓	弟				
弟	丶	丷	弓	弟	弟		

女		nǚ (299)	女	女			
		female; woman					
		女					
女	女						

妹		mèi (912)	妹	妹			
		younger sister					
		妹					
妹	女	女	女一	妅	妹	妹	

她		tā (74) she	她 她			
		她				
她	女	她				

兒 儿		ér (378) son; child	兒 儿	兒 儿		
		兒 儿				
兒	ノ	イ	仟	臼	臼	兒
儿	儿					

有		yǒu (8) to have	有 有			
		有				
有	一	ナ	有			

没		méi (51) (to have) not	没 没			
		没	没△			
没	シ	シ	汎	没		

高		gāo (105) (a surname); tall	高 高			
		高 高				
高	二	古	卢	高	高	

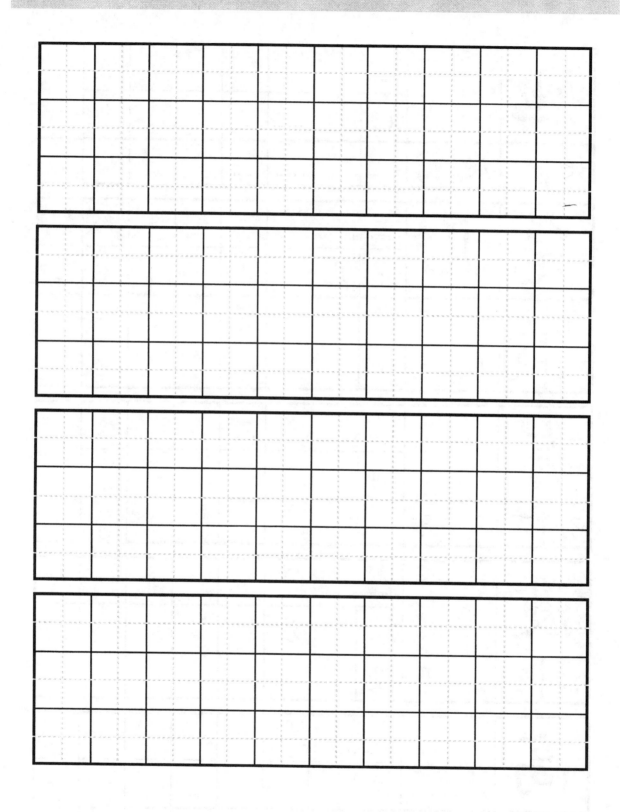

Dialogue II

家		jiā (56) family; home 家	家 家 家			
家	宀	宀	宀	穷	宛	家 家 家

幾	几	jǐ (124) how many?; a few 幾 几 幾	幾 几 几			
幾	玄	丝	絲	丝丝	丝丝	幾 幾 幾
几	丿	几				

哥		gē (489) older brother 哥	哥 哥			
哥	一	口	可	豆	哥	哥

兩	两	liǎng (103) two; a couple of 兩 两	兩 兩 兩 两			
兩	一	厂	币	帀	兩	兩
两	一	厂	冂	两	两	

和口			hé / huo (23) and / *warm			和	和			
			和							
和	ノ	禾	和							

做			zuò (168) to do; to make			做	做			
			做							
做	亻	什	估	佔	做	做	做			

英	英		yīng (915) *England; hero			英	英			
			英	英		英	英			
英	丶	十	廾	艹	苎	苎	英	英		
英	一	十	廾	艹	苎	苎	英	英		

文			wén (170) (written) language; script			文	文			
			文							
文	丶	亠	方	文						

律			lǜ (683) law; rule			律	律			
			律							
律	ノ	彳	彳	彳	律	律	律	律		

| 都 | 都 | dōu / dū (48)
all; both / capital | 都 | 都 | | | |
| | | 都 都 | | | 都 | 都 | |

| 都 | 土 | 少 | 者 | 者 | 都 | 都 | | | |
| 都 | 土 | 少 | 者 | 者 | 都 | 都 | | | |

| 醫 | 医 | yī (646)
doctor; medicine | 醫 | 醫 | | | |
| *see page 141* | | 酉 医 | | | 医 | 医 | |

醫	一	匚	工	匸	歹	矢	医	殴	殴	殴	殹
	殹	醫	醫	醫							
医	一	匚	匸	匸	歹	矢	医				

醫 醫 醫

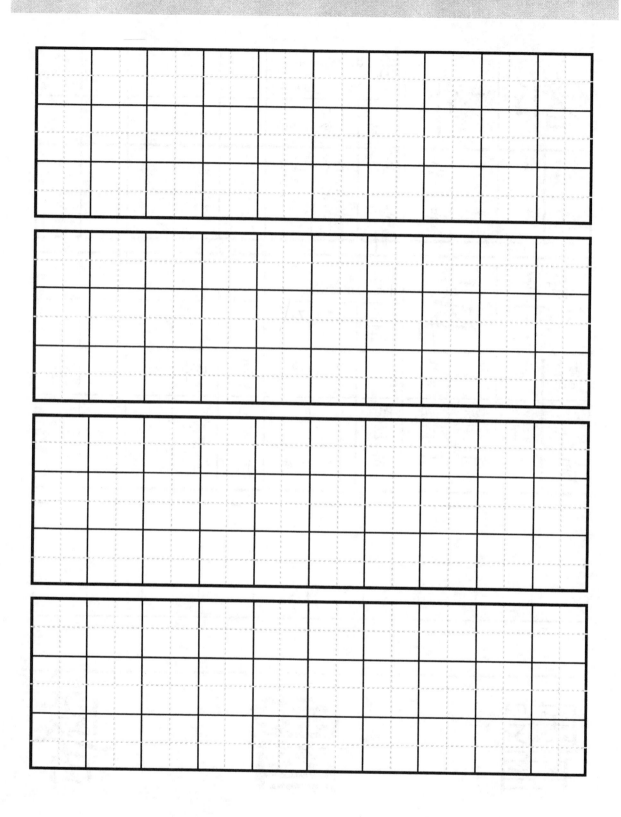

Fun With Characters

I.   CROSSWORD PUZZLE.
Fill in the squares by providing translations for the cues given below.

ACROSS
1. Who am I?
4. I have friends.
5. Teacher Wang
6   China is good.
7   What is your name?

DOWN
1. I am an American.
2. Do you have a teacher?
3. Li You is a student.

II.   RADICAL IDENTIFICATION.
Provide the Pīnyīn for each of the following characters and put the radical component each set has in common in the parentheses to the right. [Hint: Refer to the Radicals section (pp. 1-10).]

好 _____   孩 _____   李 _____   (_____)

她 _____   妹 _____   媽 (妈) _____   (_____)

他 _____   做 _____   個 (个) _____   (_____)

誰 (谁) _____   請 (请) _____   這 (这) _____   (_____)

III. MATCHING.

First, draw a line connecting the Pīnyīn to its traditional character. Then, connect the traditional character to its simplified counterpart. Finally, draw a line connecting the simplified character to its English meaning.

Pīnyīn	Traditional	Simplified	English
dōu	這	那	mom
ér	幾	張	MW (general)
ge	張	这	who
jǐ	沒	妈	son; child
liǎng	那	个	none; no
mā	兒	谁	few; several
méi	醫	儿	two
nà	誰	没	*England
shéi	都	几	all; both
yī	個	两	medicine
yīng	英	英	that
zhāng	媽	都	MW (flat objects)
zhè	兩	医	this

IV. FILL IN THE SQUARES.

Fill in each of the empty squares below with one character each that contains the radical component provided.

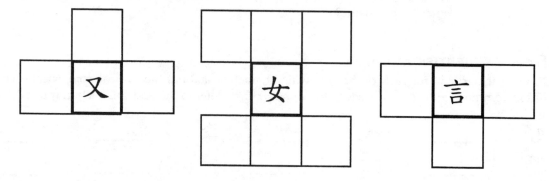

Dialogue I

月		yuè (207) month; moon	月	月			
		月					
月	月						

號 号		hào (559) number	號	號			
		號	号	号	号		
號	口	串	号	号	号	号	号	號	號
号	口	串	号				

星		xīng (499) star	星	星			
		星					
星	日	星					

期		qī (342) period (of time)	期	期			
		期					
期	一	十	廿	甘	甘	其	其	其	期

天		tiān (54) sky; heaven; day	天	天			
		天	天				
天	一	天					

		rì (269) sun; day			日	日			
日		日							
日	日								

		jīn (297) today; now			今	今			
今		今							
今	人	人	今						

		nián (49) year			年	年			
年		午	年						
年	ノ	仁	仁	仨	年	年			

		duō (53) many			多	多			
多		多							
多	夕	多							

		dà (17) big			大	大			
大		大							
大	大								

歲	岁	suì (617) age			歲	歲			
		歲	岁		岁	岁			
歲	丨	卜	屵	止	毕	产	芦	芹	芹	芹	歲
	歲	歲							
岁	丨	山	山	岁					

吃		chī (217) to eat			吃	吃			
		吃	吃	吃	吃	吃			
吃	口	口'	叱	吃	吃	吃	吃	吃	吃	吃	吃

晚	晚	wǎn (455) evening; late			晚	晚	晚	晚	晚
		晚	晚	晚	晚	晚	晚		
晚	日	日'	昈	盷	晘	晘	晘	晘	晚	晚	晚
晚	日	日'	昈	盷	晘	晘	晘	晚	晚	晚

(Please note that in the traditional form strokes 9 and 11 are two separate strokes.)

飯	饭	fàn (552) meal			飯	饭			
		飯	饭		饭	饭			
飯	飠	飠	飣	飯	饭	饭	饭	饭		
饭	饣	饣	钌	饭	饭				

怎		zěn (173) *how?		怎	怎			
		怎	怎	怎	怎	怎			
怎	⼂	⼃	⼌	乍	乍	怎	怎	怎

樣	样	yàng (70) form; kind		樣	樣			
		樣	样	樣	样			
樣	木	样	样	栏	榜	樣	樣	样
样	木	样	样	样				

太		tài (214) too; extremely		太	太			
		大						
太	大	太						

了		le / liǎo (3) P		了	了			
		了	了					
了	一	了						

樣   樣   樣

		xiè (861) to thank	謝	謝	谢	谢	
謝	谢	謝	谢		謝	謝	谢	謝
謝	言	言	言	訓	詡	詢	詢	謝	謝	谢	谢
谢	讠	讠	讠	讥	诩	讷	诮	谢	謝	

		xǐ (608) to like; happy	喜	喜	喜	喜	
喜		喜	喜	士	喜		
喜	十	士	吉	吉	吉	壹	喜			

		huān (592) joyful	歡	歡	欢	歡	
歡	欢	歡	欢		欢	欢	欢	欢
see page 141								
歡	⺿	甘	茁	藋	藋	藋	歡	歡	欢
欢	又	𡗗	𢇛	欢					

		hái / huán (45) still, yet / to return	還	還			
還	还	還	还	还	还	还		
還	罒	罒	咼	眔	睘	睘	睘	還
还	不	还						

可			kě (43)	可	可			
			but					
			可	可	可			
可	一	口	可	可				

們	们		men (12)	們	們			
			*(plural suffix)					
			們	们	们	们		
們	亻	們	们	们				
们	亻	们						

點	点		diǎn (93)	點	點			
			dot; o'clock	点	点			
			點	点				
點	丶	冂	冂	冂	回	甲	里	黑	黑	點
	點	点	黑					
点	丶	卜	占	点				

鐘	钟		zhōng (699)	鐘	鐘			
			clock					
see page 141			鐘	钟	钟	钟	钟	
鐘	金	金	釒	鉅	鈩	鈩	鐂	鐘	钟
钟	钅	钟	鐘					

半		bàn (307) half			半	半			
		半							
半	丶	丷	丷	半	半				

上		shàng (15) above; top			上	上			
		上	上	上					
上	丨	卜	上						

見 见		jiàn (101) to see			見	見			
		見	见	见	見	见			
見	目	見	見	見	见				
见	冂	贝	见						

再		zài (219) again			再	再			
		再	再	再	再	再	再		
再	一	厂	万	丙	冉	再			

白		bái (230) white			白	白			
		白							
白	丿	白							

Dialogue II

		xiàn (83)		
現	现	now	现 现	
		现 现	现 现	
现 王	现 现 现 现			
现 王 现				

		zài (7)		
在		(to be) at	在 在	
		在 在 在 在 在		
在 一 ナ 才 在				

		kè (†)		
刻		quarter hour	刻 刻	
		刻 刻 刻 刻		
刻 亥 刻				

		míng (160)		
明		bright	明 明	
		明 明 明		
明 日 明				

		máng (566)		
忙		busy	忙 忙	
		忙 忙 忙 忙		
忙 忄 忙 忙 忙				

很			hěn　　　(96) very	很	很				
			很 很 很						
很	彳	彳	彳	彳	彳	很	很		

事			shì　　　(88) matter; affair	事	事				
			亅 事 事 事						
事	一	一	彐	事					

為	为		wèi / wéi　　(39) for	為	為				
			為 为 爲	为	为				
為	丶	丿	为	为	為	為	为	丿	為
为	丶	丷	为	为	為				

(Note: The traditional character is found under radical #87, 爪, *not* #86, 火 [灬]; the simplified character is found under radical #4, 丶.)

因			yīn　　　(190) because	因	因				
			因 因 因						
因	丨	冂	因	因					

同			tóng　　　(66) same	同	同				
			同 同 同 同						
同	冂	冂	同						

認	认	rèn (294) to recognize	認	认					
		認	认		认	认			
認	言	訒	訒	認		认	认		
认	讠	认							

識	识	shí (315) to recognize	識	識					
		識	识		识	识			
see page 141									
識	言	評	諳	識	識	識	识	﹁	
识	讠	识	识	識	識				

認　認　認
識　識　識

Fun With Characters

I. SEEK AND FIND.

Hidden in the box below are some words and phrases from the text. See how many you can find and circle them. Phrases can go horizontally left to right (→), vertically top to bottom (↓), or diagonally upper left to lower right (↘) or lower left to upper right (↗).

我	們	很	忙	還	是	太	同	事
喜	你	現	在	幾	點	鐘	好	學
歡	生	明	認	識	因	為	飯	了
吃	日	十	天	明	天	晚	上	見
美	五	八	好	忙	吃	半	大	再
國	點	歲	還	你	不	多	為	見
飯	三	小	請	有	年	忙	什	樣
是	刻	我	白	今	誰	好	麼	謝
好	嗎	號	你	九	月	怎	謝	謝

II. RADICAL IDENTIFICATION.

Provide the Pīnyīn for each of the following characters and put the radical component each set has in common in the parentheses to the right. [Hint: Refer to the Radicals section (pp. 1-10).]

吃 _____   同 _____   可 _____   (_____)

太 _____   天 _____   美 _____   (_____)

明 _____   是 _____   照 _____

星 _____   都 (都) _____   晚 (晚) _____   (_____)

謝 (谢) _____   認 (认) _____   識 (识) _____   (_____)

III. MATCHING.

First, draw a line connecting the Pīnyīn to its traditional character. Then, connect the traditional character to its simplified counterpart. Finally, draw a line connecting the simplified character to its English meaning.

Pīnyīn	Traditional	Simplified	English
diǎn	們	点	number
fàn	點	谢	age
hái / huán	還	岁	evening; late
hào	謝	钟	form; kind
huān	飯	识	meal; rice
jiàn	現	为	to thank
men	晚	欢	joyful
rèn	鐘	现	still; yet
shì	號	认	*(plural suffix)
suì	識	见	dot; o'clock
wǎn	樣	样	clock
wéi / wèi	為	号	to see
xiàn	見	晚	now
xiè	歡	饭	for
yàng	認	还	to recognize
zhōng	歲	们	to recognize

IV. FILL IN THE SQUARES.

Fill in each of the empty squares below with one character that contains the radical component provided.

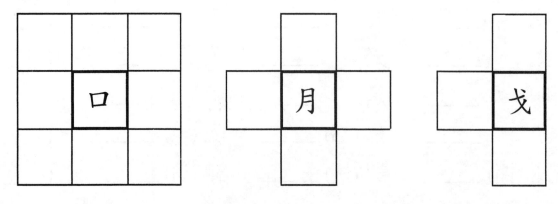

Dialogue I

		zhōu (690) week			週	週			
週	周	週	周		周	周			
週	丿	冂	円	周	週				
周	丿	冂	冃	周					

		mò (†) end			末	末			
末		末							
末	一	二	末						

		dǎ (136) to hit; to strike			打	打			
打		打							
打	扌	扩	打						

		qiú (605) ball			球	球			
球		球							
球	王	玉	玗	玙	坹	球	球	球	

		kàn (41) to watch; to look			看	看			
看		看							
看	丿	二	三	手	看				

(Please note that the first stroke goes down from right to left.)

電	电	diàn (77) electric		電	電		
		電	电	电	电		

電	雫	雪	電				
电	日	电					

視	視	shì (612) vision		視	視		
		視	视	视	视		

視	礻	視					
视	礻	视					

唱		chàng (679) to sing		唱	唱		
		唱					

唱	口	吅	唱				

歌		gē (725) song		歌	歌		
		歌					

歌	哥	歌					

| 跳 | | tiào (611) to jump | 跳 | 跳 | | | |
| 跳 足 | 趴 | 趴 | 趴 | 趴 | 跳 | 跳 | |

舞		wǔ (954) to dance; dance	舞	舞			
舞 丶	𠂉	二	仁	无	缶	血	無 舞 舞 舞
舞							

聽 听		tīng (161) to listen	聽 听	聽 听			
聽 耳	耳	耳	聽	聽	聽		
听 口	口	叮	听	听			

| 音 | | yīn (487) sound | 音 | 音 | | | |
| 音 立 | 音 | | | | | | |

樂	乐	yuè / lè (713) music / happy	樂	樂			
		樂	乐	乐	乐		
樂	白	妇	絲	樂			
乐	一	仁	乐				

對	对	duì (60) correct; right; toward	對	對			
		對	对	对	对		
對	丨	刂	刂	业	业	业	對
对	又	又	对				

時	时	shí (34) time	時	時			
		時	时	时	时		
時	日	旷	時				
时	日	时					

候		hòu (147) to wait	候	候			
		候					
候	亻	仆	伫	伫	佚	候	

書	书	shū (238) book	書 書			
		書 书		书 书		
書 書 畫 書						
书 ⁷ ⁊ 书 书						

影		yǐng (399) shadow	影 影			
		影				
影 日 旦 旦 昌 景 影						

常		cháng (202) often	常 常			
		常				
常 ⟍ ⺍ ⺌ ⺌ 尚 常						

去		qù (29) to go	去 去			
		去				
去 土 去 去						

外		wài (141) outside	外 外			
		外				
外 夕 夘 外						

客		kè (532) guest	客 客				
		客					
客	宀 宀 宇 安 客						

昨		zuó (†) yesterday	昨 昨				
		昨					
昨	日 昨						

所		suǒ (127) *so; place	所 所				
		所	所				
所	' 厂 戶 戶 所						

以		yǐ (44) with	以 以				
		以					
以	丶 ㇆ 以						

客 客 客

Dialogue II

		jiǔ (621) a long time					
久		久			久	久	
久	ノ	夕	久				

		cuò (429) wrong					
錯	错	錯	错		錯	錯	
					错	错	
錯	金	金	釒	錯			
错	钅	钅	钅	错			

		xiǎng (69) to think					
想		想			想	想	
想	木	相	想				

		jué / jiào (302) to feel / *sleep					
覺	觉	覺	觉		覺	覺	
					觉	觉	
覺	與	覺					
觉	𭣱	觉					

 覺

 覺

覺

| 得 | | | dé / děi   (28)
 to get / must
 得 | | 得 | 得 | | | |
| 得 | 亻 | 彳 | 得 | | | | | | | |

| 意 | | | yì   (122)
 meaning
 意 | | 意 | 意 | | | |
| 意 | 立 | 音 | 意 | | | | | | | |

| 思 | | | sī   (227)
 to think
 思 | | 思 | 思 | | | |
| 思 | 田 | 思 | | | | | | | | |

| 只 | | | zhǐ   (44)
 only
 只 | | 只 | 只 | | | |
| 只 | 口 | 只 | | | | | | | | |

| 睡 | | | shuì   (506)
 to sleep
 睡 | | 睡 | 睡 | | | |
| 睡 | 目 | 目 | 目 | 町 | 肝 | 睡 | 睡 | 睡 | 睡 | |

(Please note that stroke 6 goes down from right to left.)

算		suàn (334) to calculate	算	算			
算		算					
算	ノ	ノ	ゲ	竹	筲	筲	算	算

找		zhǎo (361) to look for	找	找			
找		找					
找	扌	找					

别	别	bié (167) other	别	别	别	别	
别		别	别		别	别	
别	口	另	另	别			
别	口	另	别				

算   算   算

Fun With Characters

I. CROSSWORD PUZZLE.

Fill in the squares by providing translations for the cues given below.

ACROSS

1. What time is it now?
4. Long time no see!
6. TV
7. incorrect
8. to go to bed/sleep
12. She wants to play ball.
13. What's up?
    (lit., 'Is something the matter?')
14. Why are you treating?
15. How does that sound?

DOWN

2. How many people?
3. goodbye
4. OK?
6. Watching movies is uninteresting.
7. not bad; pretty good
9. to feel; to think
10. What do you want to do?
11. Really?

II. MATCHING.

First, draw a line connecting the Pīnyīn to its traditional character. Then, connect the traditional character to its simplified counterpart. Finally, draw a line connecting the simplified character to its English meaning.

Pīnyīn	Traditional	Simplified	English
bié	書	书	wrong
cuò	視	电	week
diàn	時	对	vision
duì	電	乐	time
jué / jiào	樂	別	other
shí	別	时	music / happy
shì	錯	听	to listen
shū	對	视	to feel; *to sleep
tīng	週	周	electric
yuè / lè	聽	觉	correct; right
zhōu	覺	错	book

III. RADICAL IDENTIFICATION.

Provide the Pīnyīn for each of the following characters and put the radical component each set has in common in the parentheses to the right. [Hint: Refer to the Radicals section (pp. 1-10).]

意 _____	思 _____	想 _____	(_____)
睡 _____	算 _____	看 _____	(_____)
昨 _____	影 _____	時 (时) _____	(_____)
李 _____	樣 (样) _____	樂 (乐) _____	(_____)
得 _____	時 (时) _____	對 (对) _____	(_____)

Dialogue

呀		ya (267) P	呀	呀			
		呀					
呀	口	口丶	叮	呀	呀		

進	进	jìn (81) to enter	進	进			
		進 进	进	进			
進	隹	進					
进	一	二	于	井	进		

快		kuài (223) fast; quick(ly)	快	快			
		快					
快	忄	忙	忙	快	快		

來	来	lái (13) to come	來	来			
		來 来		來	来		
來	一	丁	对	本	來		
来	一	丷	口	立	半	来	

進　　　進　　　進

介		jiè (†) between	介	介				
		介						
介	人	个	介					

紹	绍	shào (†) to carry on; continue	紹	绍			
		紹	绍	绍	绍		
紹	纟	紹	紹				
绍	纟	绍	绍				

下		xià (36) below; under	下	下				
		下						
下	一	丁	下					

興	兴	xìng (†) mood; interest	興	兴			
		興	兴	兴	兴		
興	ﾁ	同	同	興	興		
兴	ﾂ	兴	兴				

漂		piào (†) *pretty*		漂	漂			
		漂						
漂	シ	ジ	ジ	沪	沪	涄	涄	漂

亮 亮		liàng (538) bright		亮	亮			
		亮	亮	亮	亮			
亮	亠	古	古	亮				
亮	亠	古	古	亮				

坐		zuò (371) to sit		坐	坐		
		坐					
坐	人	从	坐				

哪 哪		nǎ / něi (275) QW; which?; where?		哪	哪		
		口哪	哪	哪	哪		
哪	口	叨	哪	哪	哪		
哪	口	叨	哪	哪			

哪　　　哪　　　哪

工		gōng (55) craft 工		工 工			
工 工							

作		zuò (214) to work; to do 作		作 作			
作 亻 作							

校		xiào (636) school 校		校 校			
校 木 杧 校							

喝		hē (720) to drink 喝		喝 喝			
喝 口 叩 叩 喝 喝 喝							

茶 茶		chá (985) tea 茶 茶		茶 茶			
茶 亠 艹 艾 茶							
茶 艹 艾 茶							

咖		kā (†) *coffee	咖	咖			
		口咖					
咖	口	叻	咖						

啡		fēi (†) *coffee	啡	啡			
		口啡					
啡	口	叮	叮	吲	唎	啡	

啤		pí (†) *beer	啤	啤			
		口啤					
啤	口	口'	吖	叻	吶	咱	啤	啤

酒		jiǔ (858) wine	酒	酒			
		酒	酒				
酒	氵	酒					

吧		ba (175) P	吧	吧			
		口吧					
吧	口	吧					

要			yào (25) to want	要	要			
			要					
要	覀	要						

杯			bēi (†) cup; glass	杯	杯			
			杯	盃△				
杯	木	杯						

起			qǐ (47) to rise	起	起			
			起					
起	土	走	起	起	起			

給	给		gěi (114) to give	給	给	給	给	
			給	给	給	给		
給	糹	糹	糹	給				
给	纟	纟	纟	给				

水			shuǐ (102) water	水	水			
			水					
水	丿	才	水	水				

Narrative

玩		wán (970) to have a visit; to play		玩	玩			
		玩						
玩	王	玗	玩					

圖	图	tú (7) drawing		圖	圖			
see page 142		圖	图	图	图			
圖	冂	冂	冏	周	圖	圖	圖	
图	冂	冂	冈	冈	图	图	图	

館	馆	guǎn (938) accomodations		館	館			
		館	馆		馆	馆		
館	飠	飩	飩	節	節	館		
馆	饣	馆	馆	馆	馆	馆		

瓶		píng (†) bottle		瓶	瓶			
		瓶						
瓶	丶	丷	丷	兰	关	并	并	荓	瓶	瓶

聊		liáo (†) to chat	聊	聊			
		聊					
聊	耳	耳	耳	耴	聊	聊	

才		cái (162) not until	才	才			
		才	才				
才	一	寸	才				

(Note: The traditional character is found under radical #64, 手 [扌])

回		huí (108) to return	回	回			
		回					
回	冂	向	回				

聊   聊

Fun With Characters

I. SEEK AND FIND.

Hidden in the box below are some words and phrases from the text. See how many you can find and circle them. Phrases can go horizontally left to right (→), vertically top to bottom (↓), or diagonally upper left to lower right (↘) or lower left to upper right (↗).

玩	認	識	你	很	高	興	茶	我
今	天	下	午	我	要	開	會	在
介	水	漂	坐	學	下	咖	給	圖
想	紹	請	亮	一	校	啡	作	書
王	坐	好	瓶	打	起	工	王	館
請	老	來	看	球	兒	樂	朋	工
客	進	師	聽	哪	可	只	喝	作
快	別	請	在	回	才	以	啤	吧
誰	呀	你	進	嗎	家	找	酒	杯

II. RADICAL IDENTIFICATION.

Provide the Pīnyīn for each of the following characters and put the radical component each set has in common in the parentheses to the right. [Hint: Refer to the Radicals section (pp. 1-10).]

做	_____	作	_____	坐	_____	(_____)
忙	_____	快	_____	想	_____	(_____)
漂	_____	酒	_____	没 (沒) _____		(_____)
因	_____	回	_____	圖 (图) _____		(_____)
覺 (觉) _____		視 (视) _____		現 (现) _____		(_____)

III. MATCHING.

First, draw a line connecting the Pīnyīn to its traditional character. Then, connect the traditional character to its simplified counterpart. Finally, draw a line connecting the simplified character to its English meaning.

Pīnyīn	Traditional	Simplified	English
chá	來	进	accomodations
gěi	亮	来	mood; interest
guǎn	茶	绍	to continue
jìn	哪	兴	drawing
lái	紹	亮	to enter
liàng	給	哪	to come
nǎ	進	茶	to give
shào	圖	给	which
tú	館	图	bright
xìng	興	馆	tea

IV. FILL IN THE SQUARES.

Fill in each of the empty squares below with one character each **from this lesson only** that contains the radical component provided.

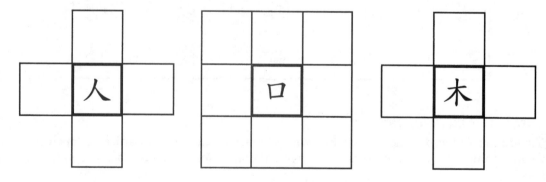

Dialogue I

話	话	huà (137) speech 話 话		話	话				
話 言 言 訴 話										
话 讠 讠 讠 话										

喂		wèi (†) Hello!; Hey! 喂		喂	喂				
喂 口 吧 吧 吧 喂										

就		jiù (19) then 就 就		就	就				
就 丶 二 古 京 京 献 就 就										

位		wèi (†) M (polite, people) 位		位	位				
位 亻 位										

午		wǔ (882) noon 午 午		午	午				
午 丿 ㇒ 午										

間	间	jiān　　　　(156)　M (for rooms)	間	间			
		間	间		间	间	
間	門	間					
间	门	间					

題	题	tí　　　　(224)　topic; question	題	题			
		題	题		題	题	
題	是	是	是	題	题		
題	是	是	是	題			

開	开	kāi　　　　(94)　to open; to hold	開	开			
		開	开		开	开	
開	門	開					
开	开						

會	会	huì　　　　(32)　to meet	會	會			
see page 142		會	会		会	会	
會	人	人	今	合	侖	侖	侖	會
会	人	仝	会	会			

節	节	jié (555) M (for classes)	節	节	節 节		
		節 节			节 节		
節	⺮	竺	竻	笃	笚	筤	節
节	⺿	芍	节				

課	课	kè (762) class; lesson	課	课	課 课		
		課 课			課 课		
課	言	訂	課				
课	讠	训	课				

級	级	jí (172) level; rank	級	级	級 级		
		級 级			級 级		
級	糸	糿	紉	紗	級		
级	纟	纠	级	级			

考		kǎo (767) to give or take a test	考	考		
		考				
考	土	耂	耂	考		

(Note: This character is found under the traditional radical #125 and the simplified radical #133, 老).

試	试	shì (701)	試	試			
		to try; to test					
		試	试		試	試	
試	言	訁	訁	試	試		
试	讠	订	证	试	试		

後	后	hòu (73)	後	後			
		after; behind; rear					
		後	后		后	后	
後	彳	彳	彳	後			
后	ノ	厂	广	后			

空		kòng (340)	空	空			
		free time					
		空					
空	宀	宀	穴	空			

方		fāng (96)	方	方			
		square					
		方					
方	丶	亠	方	方			

後   後   後

便		biàn / pián (282) convenient / *cheap	便	便			
		便					
便	亻	仁	佢	便	便		

到		dào (22) to go to; to arrive	到	到			
		到					
到	一	工	互	至	到		

辦	办	bàn (313) to manage	辦	辦			
		辦 办	办	办			
辦	立	产	辛	辡	辦	辦	
办	力	力	办				

公		gōng (259) public	公	公			
		公					
公	八	公					

室		shì (669) room	室	室			
		室					
室	宀	宀	宔	宰	室		

| 行 | | xíng / háng   (99) be all right; OK / firm | 行 | 行 | | | |
| 行 | 彳 | 仁 | 仃 | 行 | | | | |

| 等 | | děng   (35) to wait | 等 | 等 | | | |
| 等 | 竹 | 竿 | 等 | | | | | |

氣	气	qì air	氣 气	氣 气	氣 气		
氣	ノ	⺈	⺅	气	气	氙	氙	氘	氣	氣
气	ノ	⺈	⺅	气						

氣   氣   氣

Dialogue II

幫 see page 142	帮	bāng (536) to help	幫 帮	幫	幫		
			帛 巾	帮	帮		
幫	土	圭	封	責	幫		
帮	三	丰	邦	帮			

練 see page 142	练	liàn (950) to drill	練 练	練	練			
					练	练		
練	幺	糸	糸	紳	糸	緬	紳	練
练	纟	纟	纟	纬	练			

習	习	xí (11) to practice	習 习	習	習		
					习	习	
習	ヲ	ヲ	习	羽	習		
习	フ	ヨ	习				

説	说	shuō (21) to speak	説 说	説	説		
					说	说	
説	言	言	討	話	説		
说	讠	访	访	诮	说		

啊	啊	a (254) P			啊	啊			
		啊	啊		啊	啊			
啊	口	口	叮	吓	啊				
啊	口	叮	吓	啊					

但		dàn (150) but			但	但		
		但						
但	亻	伃	但					

知		zhī (131) to know			知	知		
		知						
知	矢	知						

道	道	dào (78) path; way			道	道		
		道	道		道	道		
道	⺍	丷	丷	首	道			
道	⺍	丷	丷	首	道			

道   道   道

Fun With Characters

I. CROSSWORD PUZZLE.

Fill in the squares by providing translations for the cues given below.

ACROSS
1. last weekennd
3. afternoon
4. What do you want to watch?
6. together
7. five o'clock
9. (do you) have free time?
11. several questions

DOWN
1. morning
2. when (do you) have free time?
3. next Friday
5. watch a movie
6. one minute
8. a bit; some
10. no problem

II. RADICAL IDENTIFICATION.

Provide the Pīnyīn for each of the following characters and put the radical component each set has in common in the parentheses to the right. [Hint: Refer to the Radicals section (pp. 1-10).]

喂 _____   吧 _____   啊 (啊) _____   (_____)

级 (级) _____   給 (给) _____   練 (练) _____   (_____)

開 (开) _____   間 (间) _____   問 (问) _____   (_____)

説 (说) _____   話 (话) _____   試 (试) _____   (_____)

III. MATCHING.

First, draw a line connecting the Pīnyīn to its traditional character. Then, connect the traditional character to its simplified counterpart. Finally, draw a line connecting the simplified character to its English meaning.

Pīnyīn	Traditional	Simplified	English
a	級	題	after; rear; behind
bàn	氣	道	air
bāng	間	課	class; lesson
dào	開	啊	level; rank
hòu	辦	说	M (for classes)
huà	題	帮	M (for rooms)
huì	後	试	P
jí	啊	练	path; way
jiān	習	话	speech
jié	道	间	topic; question
kāi	會	级	to drill
kè	話	会	to help
liàn	節	后	to manage
qì	試	节	to meet
shì	說	气	to open; to hold
shuō	課	开	to practice
tí	練	办	to speak
xí	幫	习	to try; to test

IV. PHONOLOGICAL DISTINCTION.

Provide the full Pīnyīn (including tone) for each of the following characters and then put the basic homonym (initial + final, but no tone) each set shares in the parentheses to the right.

七 _____   起 _____   氣 (气)_____   (___)

九 _____   久 _____   就 _____   (___)

十 _____   室 _____   試 (试)_____   (___)

Dialogue I

		gēn (247) with; to follow; and 跟	跟	跟			
跟	足	跟					

		zhù (632) to assist 助	助	助			
助	且	助					

		fù (525) duplicate 復 复	復	復			
復	彳	彳	铂	復		復	復
复	𠂉	𠂤	复			复	复

		xiě (317) to write 寫 写	寫	寫			
寫	宀	宭	寫	寫		写	写
写	冖	冖	写	写			

寫

慢		màn (657) slow		慢	慢				
		慢							
慢	忄	忸	惺	慢					

教		jiāo / jiào (244) to teach / education		教	教				
		教	敎△						
教	土	耂	孝	孝	孝	教	教		

筆	笔	bǐ (775) pen		筆	筆				
		筆	笔	笔	笔				
筆	竹	筆							
笔	竹	竺	笔						

難	难	nán (285) difficult		難	難				
		難	难	难	难				
see page 142									
難	一	十	廿	廿	苩	莒	菓	難	
难	又	难							

難　難　難

		lǐ (26)		裏	裏			
	里	inside						
裏		裏 裡 里		里	里			

裏	一	重	裏
裡	礻	裡	
里	里		

(Note: The standard form and the variant form of this character are completely interchangeable.)

	dì (211)		第	第			
第	(ordinal prefix)						
	第						

| 第 | ⺮ | 第 |

		yù (892)		預	預			
預	预	to prepare						
		預 预		預	預			

| 預 | ⁊ | ⁊ | 予 | 予 | 預 |
| 预 | ⁊ | ⁊ | 予 | 予 | 预 |

		yǔ (706)		語	語			
語	语	language						
		語 语		語	语			

| 語 | 言 | 語 | 語 |
| 语 | 讠 | 语 | 语 |

法		fǎ　　　　　(142) method; way	法	法			
		法					
法	氵	法					

容		róng　　　　(421) hold; contain; allow	容	容			
		容					
容	宀	宀	灾	容			

易		yì　　　　　(582) easy	易	易			
		易					
易	日	昌	易	易			

懂	懂	dǒng　　　　(269) to understand	懂	懂			
		懂	懂				
懂	忄	忙	忪	忰	惜	懂	懂
懂	忄	忙	忪	忰	惜	懂	懂

懂　　　　懂　　　　懂

		cí (†) word		詞	詞			
詞	词	詞	词		詞	词		

詞	言	訂	訂	詞				
词	讠	订	订	词				

		hàn (†) Chinese		漢	漢			
漢	汉	漢	汉		汉	汉		

漢	氵	漢						
汉	氵	汉						

詞　　　詞　　　詞

漢　　　漢　　　漢

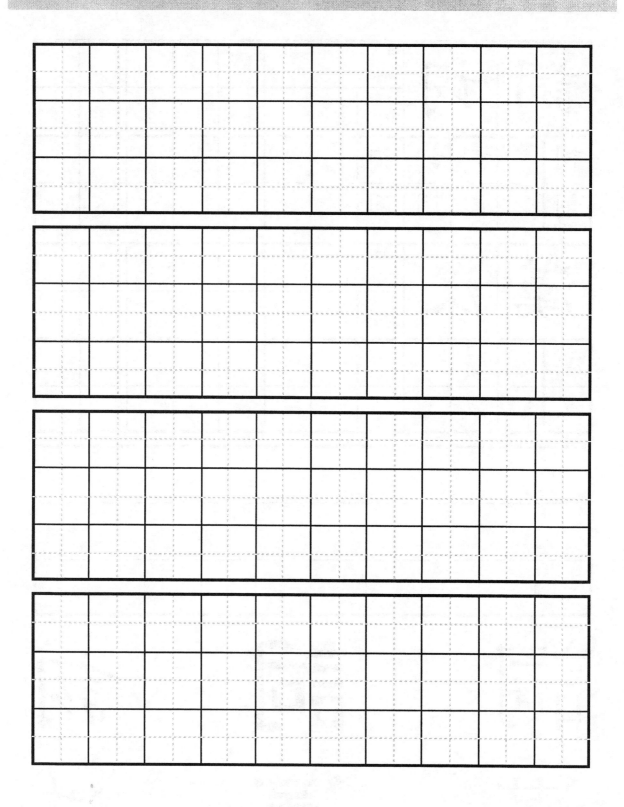

Dialogue II

平		píng (232) level; even		平	平		
		平	平				
平	一	ㄧ	彐	立	平		

早		zǎo (344) early		早	早		
		早					
早	日	早					

夜		yè (405) night		夜	夜		
		夜	夜				
夜	亠	亣	疒	疠	夜	夜	

功		gōng (681) skill		功	功		
		功					
功	工	功					

真		zhēn (159) true; real(ly)		真	真		
		真	真	眞			
真	一	ナ	广	方	直	直	真

始			shǐ (548) to begin	始	始			
			始					
始	女	女	始					

唸	念		niàn (620) to read (aloud)	唸	唸			
			口	念	念	念		
唸	口	吟	唸					
念	今	念						

(See Preface, p. iii)

錄	录		lù (†) to record	錄	录			
			錄	录		录	录	
錄	金	釒	鈩	鈩	鈩	鈩	錄	
录	フ	ヨ	ヨ	寻	寻	录		

帥	帅		shuài (†) handsome; smart	帥	帥			
			帥	帅		帅	帅	
帥	皀	帥						
帅	リ	帅						

Fun With Characters

I. SEEK AND FIND.

Hidden in the box below are some words and phrases from the text. See how many you can find and circle them. Phrases can go horizontally left to right (→), vertically top to bottom (↓), or diagonally upper left to lower right (↘) or lower left to upper right (↗).

客	中	國	朋	友	有	漢	寫	圖
上	個	星	期	午	一	電	字	子
課	功	課	公	五	點	謝	寫	難
氣	七	唸	年	室	兒	寫	得	快
第	哪	知	課	道	王	朋	很	帥
生	夜	女	男	文	考	錄	好	音
級	詞	考	試	考	得	怎	麼	樣
練	預	太	助	平	不	半	始	這
復	習	學	多	瓶	錯	辦	怎	麼

II. RADICAL IDENTIFICATION.

Provide the Pīnyīn for each of the following characters and put the radical component each set has in common in the parentheses to the right. [Hint: Refer to the Radicals section (pp. 1-10).]

早 _____   易 _____   復 (复) _____   (_____)

始 _____   知 _____   亮 (亮) _____   (_____)

難 (难) _____   誰 (谁) _____   進 (进) _____   (_____)

詞 (词) _____   語 (语) _____   話 (话) _____   (_____)

III. MATCHING.

First, draw a line connecting the Pīnyīn to its traditional character. Then, connect the traditional character to its simplified counterpart. Finally, draw a line connecting the simplified character to its English meaning.

Pīnyīn	Traditional	Simplified	English
bǐ	預	汉	to duplicate
cí	裏	帅	to write
dǒng	復	写	pen
fù	詞	词	difficult
hàn	筆	里	inside
lǐ	唸	录	to prepare
lù	帥	念	language
nán	難	复	to understand
niàn	懂	语	word
shuài	錄	笔	Chinese
xiě	寫	难	to read
yǔ	語	预	to record
yù	漢	懂	handsome

IV. FILL IN THE SQUARES.

Fill in each of the empty squares below with one character each that contains the radical component provided.

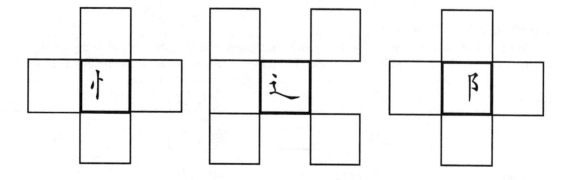

Dialogue I

篇		piān (†) M (for articles) 篇	篇	篇				
篇	竺	竺	笁	笁	笁	笃	笃	篇

記	记	jì (289) record; to remember 記 记	記 记 记 记					
記 言 記								
记 讠 记								

床		chuáng (682) bed 床 牀△	床 床					
床 广 床								

洗		xǐ (860) to wash 洗	洗 洗					
洗 氵 洗								

澡		zǎo (†) bath 澡	澡 澡					
澡 氵 氵 氵 澡 澡								

邊	边	biān (140) side	邊	邊			
see page 136		邊	边		边	边		
邊	自	島	鼻	邊				
边	力	边						

發	发	fā (64) to emit; to issue	發	發			
		發	发		发	发		
發	㇇	㇖	㇖	癶	癸	發		
发	㇉	㇉	发	发				

新		xīn (181) new	新	新			
		新						
新	立	亲	新					

腦	脑	nǎo (600) brain	腦	腦			
		腦	脑		脑	脑		
腦	月	肜	肜	肜	脳	脳	腦	腦
脑	月	肜	胶	脑	脑			

餐		cān (†)	餐	餐			
		meal					
see page 143		餐					
餐	⺈	⺈	⼣	⿰	餐		

廳	厅	tīng (†)	廳	廳			
		hall	廳	厅	厅	厅	
see page 143							
廳	广	廳					
厅	厂	厅					

報	报	bào (333)	報	报			
		newspaper	報	报	报	报	
報	土	去	吉	幸	刲	郣	報
报	扌	扪	护	报			

宿		sù (†)	宿	宿			
		to stay	宿				
宿	宀	宀	宀	宿			

廳　　廳　　廳

舍		shè house	(†)	舍	舍			
		舍						
舍	人	人	会	今	舍			

正		zhèng just	(†)	正	正			
		正						
正	一	丁	下	正	正			

前		qián front; before	(91)	前	前			
		前						
前	丶	丷	丷	首	前			

告		gào to tell; to inform	(346)	告	告			
		告						
告	生	告						

訴	诉	sù to tell; to relate	(545)	訴	诉			
		訴	诉					
訴	言	訴	訴					
诉	讠	诉	诉					

已		yǐ (171) already	已	已			
		已					
已	フ	コ	已					

經 经		jīng (76) pass through	經	經			
		經	经		經	經	
					经	经	
經	糸	糸	經	經			
经	纟	纟	纟	经			

已　　　　已　　　　已

經　　　　經　　　　經

Dialogue II

封		fēng (689) M (for letters) 封	封 封			
封	土	圭	封			

信		xìn (318) letter 信	信 信			
信	亻	信				

最		zuì (174) (superalative); most 最	最 最			
最	日	昌	最			

(Note: This character is under traditional radical #73 and simplified radical #83, 日.)

近 近		jìn (414) near 近 近	近 近			
近	斤	近				
近	斤	近				

最 最 最

除	除	chú (562) except			除	除			
		除	除		除	除			
除	阝	队	队	除					
除	阝	队	队	除					

專	专	zhuān (519) special			專	專			
		專	专		专	专			
專	一	百	車	重	重	專			
专	二	专	专						

業	业	yè (562) occupation; profession			業	業			
		業	业		业	业			
業	业	业	业	丵	掌	業			
业	业								

慣	惯	guàn (†) to be used to			慣	慣			
		慣	惯		慣	慣			
慣	忄	忄	忄	忄	忄	慣			
惯	忄	忄	忄	忄	忄	惯			

清			qīng (381) clear; clean 清		清	清			
清	氵	泔	清						

楚			chǔ (907) clear; neat 楚		楚	楚			
楚	木	林	栊	棥	楚	楚	楚		

步			bù (314) step 步		步	步			
步	卜	山	止	步					

希			xī (818) to hope 希		希	希			
希	メ	孑	希						

望	望		wàng (298) to hope; to expect 望	望	望	望			
望	亡	七	切	切	竘	望			
望	亡	胡	望						

能		néng (52) to be able	能 能		
		能			
能	ㄥ	自	能	能	

用		yòng (59) to use	用 用		
		用			
用	丿	冂	月	用	

笑		xiào (250) to laugh	笑 笑		
		笑			
笑	𥫗	竺	笑		

祝		zhù (†) to wish	祝 祝		
		祝			
祝	礻	祀	祝		

笑   笑   笑

Fun With Characters

I. CROSSWORD PUZZLE.

Fill in the squares by providing translations for the cues given below.

ACROSS

1. (along with 1 Down, indicates two simultaneous actions)
3. Who are you?
5. What do you think (feel)?
6. eat breakfast after bathing
8. What would you like to do?
10. 6:30
11. one good class
13. go together
15. long time no see

DOWN

1. see 1 Across
2. do homework before going to bed
4. Who's cooking?
7. what time (did you) get up?
9. wait a moment
12. (is it) OK?
14. good-bye

II. RADICAL IDENTIFICATION.

Provide the Pīnyīn for each of the following characters and put the radical component each set has in common in the parentheses to the right. [Hint: Refer to the Radicals section (pp. 1-10).]

洗 _____	澡 _____	清 _____	(___)
餐 _____	飯 (饭) _____	館 (馆) _____	(___)
經 (经) _____	給 (给) _____	練 (练) _____	(___)
們 (们) _____	間 (间) _____	問 (问) _____	(___)

III. MATCHING.

First, draw a line connecting the Pīnyīn to its traditional character. Then, connect the traditional character to its simplified counterpart. Finally, draw a line connecting the simplified character to its English meaning.

Pīnyīn	Traditional	Simplified	English
bào	記	厅	hall
biān	邊	专	side
chú	發	边	near
fā	腦	发	brain
guàn	廳	记	except
jì	報	业	record
jìn	訴	诉	special
jīng	經	报	occupation
nǎo	近	近	newspaper
sù	除	经	to be used to
tīng	專	除	to tell; to relate
wàng	業	脑	to pass through
yè	慣	望	to emit; to issue
zhuān	望	惯	to hope; to expect

IV. PHONOLOGICAL DISTINCTION.

Provide the full Pīnyīn (including tone) for each of the following characters and then put the basic homonym (initial + final, but no tone) each set shares in the parentheses to the right.

一	＿＿	已	＿＿	意	＿＿	(＿＿)
五	＿＿	午	＿＿	舞	＿＿	(＿＿)
七	＿＿	起	＿＿	期	＿＿	(＿＿)
八	＿＿	吧	＿＿	爸	＿＿	(＿＿)
九	＿＿	酒	＿＿	就	＿＿	(＿＿)
十	＿＿	始	＿＿	是	＿＿	(＿＿)

Dialogue I

		măi (460) to buy						
買	买	買 买		買 買				
買	罒 買							
买	一 ㄱ ㄥ 买							

		dōng (234) east						
東	东	東 东		东 东				
東	一 百 車 東							
东	一 匕 东							

		xī (225) west						
西		西		西 西				
西	西							

		shòu (†) to sell						
售		售		售 售				
售	佳 售							

貨 货	货	huò　　　　(773) merchandise			货	货			
		貝	货		货	货			
貨	亻	化	貨						
貨	亻	化	貨						

員 员	员	yuán　　　　(200) personnel			員	員			
		員	员		员	员			
員	口	員							
员	口	员							

衣		yī　　　　(473) clothing			衣	衣			
		衣							
衣	衣								

服		fú　　　　(375) clothing			服	服			
		服							
服	月	服							

貨

件		jiàn (311) M (for items)	件	件			
		件					
件	亻	伫	仵	件			

襯	衬	chèn (†) lining	襯	襯			
		襯	衬	襯	衬		
襯	衤	衬	襟	襯			
衬	衤	衬					

see page 143

衫		shān (†) shirt	衫	衫			
		衫					
衫	衤	衫					

顏	颜	yán (†) face; countenance	顏	顏			
		顏	颜	顏	颜		
顏	文	产	彦	顏			
颜	立	产	彦	颜			

see page 143

襯　　　襯　　　襯

色		sè (287) color	色	色			
		色	色				
色	ノ	ク	色				

黄		huáng (638) yellow	黄	黄			
		黄	黄	黄△			
黄	一	サ	世	艿	苎	苗	苗	黄

紅	红	hóng (352) red	紅	紅			
		紅	红		紅	紅	
紅	糸	紅					
红	纟	红					

穿		chuān (539) to wear	穿	穿			
		穿					
穿	穴	穿					

黄   黄   黄

		tiáo (213)					
條	条	M (for long objects)	條	條			
		條 条		条 条			
條	亻	伫	攸	條			
条	ノ	夂	条				

		kù (†)					
褲	裤	pants	褲	褲			
see page 143		褲 裤		褲 褲			
褲	衤	衤	衤	裆	裆	褲	
裤	衤	衤	衤	裆	裆	裤	

		yí (†)					
宜		suitable; *cheap	宜	宜			
		宜					
宜	宀	宜					

		fù (†)					
付		to pay	付	付			
		付					
付	亻	付					

褲 褲 褲

		qián (398)		錢	錢			
錢	钱	money						
		錢	钱		錢	钱		
錢	金	銭	錢					
钱	钅	针	钱					

		gòng (283)		共	共			
共		altogether						
		共						
共	丑	共						

		shǎo (192)		少	少			
少		few						
		少						
少	小	少						

		kuài (403)		塊	塊			
塊	块	piece; dollar						
		塊	块		块	块		
塊	土	圠	坤	塊	塊			
块	土	块						

錢   錢   錢

毛		máo (531) hair; dime	毛 毛			
		毛				
毛	ノ	二	三	毛		

分		fēn (90) penny; minute	分 分			
		分				
分	八	分				

百		bǎi (233) hundred	百 百			
		白				
百	一	百				

百　　百　　百

Dialogue II

		shuāng (729) M; pair	雙	雙				
雙	双	雙 双	双	双				
雙	隹	雔	雙					
双	又	双						

		xié (901) shoe	鞋	鞋				
鞋		鞋						
鞋	廿	莒	莒	革	鞋	鞋		

		huàn (745) to (ex)change	換	換				
換	换	換 换	換	换				
換	扌	扩	抈	抈	捄	換		
换	扌	扩	抈	换				

		hēi (438) black	黑	黑				
黑		黑						
黑	罜	黑						

雙 雙 雙

雖	虽	suí (603) though	雞	雞			
		雖 虽	虽	虽			
雞	口	呂	吊	虽	虽	雞	
虽	口	呂	吊	虽	虽		

然		rán (84) like that; so	然	然			
		然					
然	ク	タ	夕	外	然	然	

合		hé (215) to suit; to agree	合	合			
		合					
合	人	人	合				

適	适	shì (757) to suit; to fit	適	適			
		適 适	适	适			
適	一	六	肖	商	適		
适	丿	舌	适				

雖   雖   雖

Fun With Characters

I. SEEK AND FIND.

Hidden in the box below are some words and phrases from the text. See how many you can find and circle them. Phrases can go horizontally left to right (→), vertically top to bottom (↓), or diagonally upper left to lower right (↘) or lower left to upper right (↗).

服	襪	員	長	不	賣	樣	衣	兒
很	貨	我	想	買	一	件	襯	衫
售	便	王	多	外	百	共	灰	咖
裝	謝	宜	毛	少	塊	清	紅	啡
戴	在	哪	兒	付	錢	顏	黑	色
短	麼	大	雖	找	然	小	黃	希
太	李	小	姐	穿	中	號	的	西
貴	分	合	經	大	訴	好	東	帽
了	換	適	室	張	用	買	裙	子

II. RADICAL IDENTIFICATION.

Provide the Pīnyīn for each of the following characters and put the radical component each set has in common in the parentheses to the right. [Hint: Refer to the Radicals section (pp. 1-10).]

然	_____	黑	_____	點 (点) _____	(_____)
售	_____	雙	_____	雖 (虽) _____	(_____)
封	_____	鞋	_____	塊 (块) _____	(_____)
襯 (衬) _____		衫	_____	褲 (裤) _____	(_____)
貨 (货) _____		員 (员) _____		買 (买) _____	(_____)

III. MATCHING.

First, draw a line connecting the Pīnyīn to its traditional character. Then, connect the traditional character to its simplified counterpart. Finally, draw a line connecting the simplified character to its English meaning.

<u>Pīnyīn</u>	<u>Traditional</u>	<u>Simplified</u>	<u>English</u>
chèn	買	颜	to buy
dōng	東	裤	to (ex)change
hóng	貨	钱	to suit; to fit
huàn	員	换	countenance
huò	襯	虽	east
kù	顏	适	lining
kuài	紅	货	merchandise
mǎi	條	衬	money
qián	褲	员	pants
shì	錢	条	personnel
shuāng	塊	块	piece; dollar
suī	雙	买	red
tiáo	換	红	M; pair
yán	雖	东	M (for long objects)
yuán	適	双	though

IV. FILL IN THE SQUARES.

Fill in each of the empty squares below with one character each **from this lesson only** that contains the radical component provided.

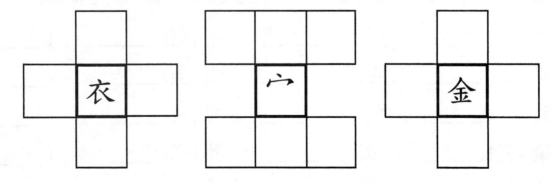

Dialogue I

比		bǐ (206) to compare 比		比	比				
比	一	上	比						

雨		yǔ (542) rain 雨		雨	雨				
雨	雨								

更		gèng (260) even more 更 更		更	更				
更	一	曰	更	更					

而		ér (95) and; in addition 而 而		而	而				
而	一	丆	广	丙	而	而			

且		qiě (355) for the time being 且		且	且				
且	且								

暖		nuǎn (†) warm			暖	暖			
		暖							
暖	日	旷	旷	旷	旷	旷	暖		

約	约	yuē (568) to make an appointment			約	約			
		約	约		約	约			
約	纟	約							
约	纟	约							

園	园	yuán (898) garden			園	園			
		園	园		园	园			
園	l	冂	冏	周	園	園			
园	l	冂	元	园					

葉	叶	yè (777) leaf			葉	葉			
		葉	叶		叶	叶			
葉	⺿	芷	葉						
叶	口	叶							

像	像	xiàng (†) image; to resemble	像	像		像	像				
		像	像			像	像				
像	亻	伫	伃	伃	伃	像					
像	亻	伫	伃	像							

海		hǎi (348) sea	海	海				
		海						
海	氵	氵	汸	海	海	海	海	

像　　　像　　　像

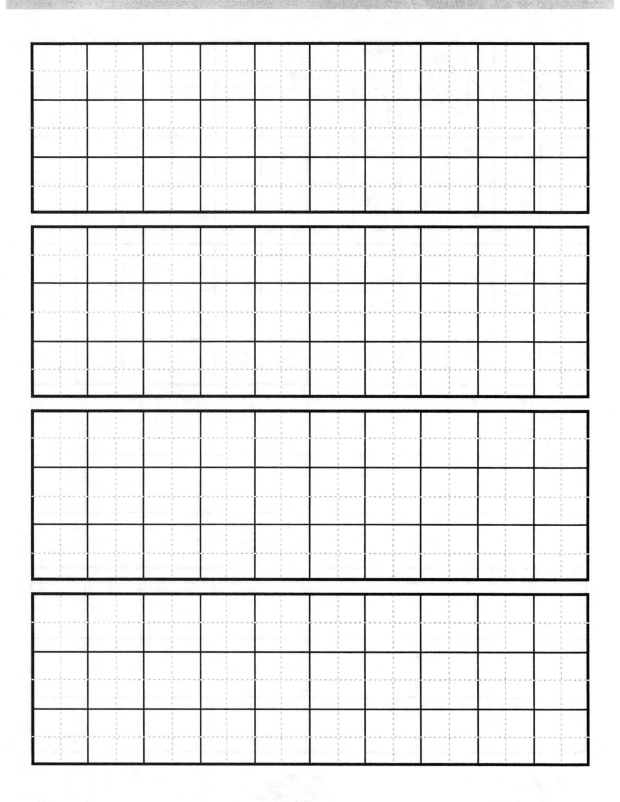

Dialogue II

糟		zāo *(†)* messy; in a mess	糟	糟				
see page 144		糟							
糟	米	米	粓	粬	糟	糟	糟		

糕		gāo *(†)* cake	糕	糕				
		糕							
糕	米	糀	糕						

又		yòu *(65)* again	又	又				
		又							
又	又								

剛	刚	gāng *(415)* just now	剛	剛				
		剛	刚	剛	刚				
剛	冂	冈	冈	岡	剛				
刚	冂	冈	刚						

出		chū *(35)* to go out	出	出				
		出							
出	乚	屮	屮	出					

		rè (319) hot	热	热			
熱	热	热	热	热	热		
熱	土	夫	坴	執	執	熱	
热	扌	执	热				

		shū (†) to stretch; to relax	舒	舒			
舒			舒				
舒	人	全	舍	舒			

		xià (†) summer	夏	夏			
夏			夏				
夏	一	百	夏				

		liáng (†) cool	涼	涼			
涼	涼	涼	涼	涼	涼		
涼	氵	涼					
涼	冫	涼					

熱　熱　熱

| 春 | | chūn (736)
spring | 春 | 春 春 | | |
| 春 三 丰 夫 春 | | 春 | | | | |

| 冬 | | dōng (†)
winter | 冬 冬 | 冬 冬 | | |
| 冬 夂 冬 冬 | | | | | | |

| 冷 | | lěng (587)
cold | 冷 | 冷 冷 | | |
| 冷 丶 冫 冷 冷 | | | | | | |

悶 悶		mēn (†) stuffy	悶 闷	悶 悶 闷 闷		
悶 門 悶						
闷 门 闷						

| 次 | | cì (210)
M (for occurrences) | 次 | 次 次 | | |
| 次 冫 次 | | | | | | |

秋		qiū (†) autumn; fall		秋	秋			
		秋						
秋	禾	秋						

台		tái (526) platform; stage		台	台			
		台	臺△					
台	厶	台						

北		běi (464) north		北	北			
		北	北					
北	丨	十	丬	北				

灣 湾 see page 144		wān (†) strait; bay		灣	湾		灣	灣
		灣	湾				湾	湾
灣	氵	浐	澬	澸	灣			
湾	氵	宀	汢	汻	沭	湾		

Fun With Characters

I. CROSSWORD PUZZLE.

Fill in the squares by providing translations for the cues given below.

ACROSS

1. Are you going?
5. summer is **both** hot **and** stuffy
7. 19th
9. incorrect (new situation)
10. June is not cold.
12. good (new situation)
13. tomorrow
14. Will that do?
16. ... **but** it will **also** be a bit warmer
19. next time
20. China
21. What is your surname?

DOWN

2. gone for 16 days
3. winter is very cold
4. too hot (now)
6. wrong again
8. September
11. **not only** will it not rain ...
12. OK?
13. next year
15. to chat
17. as expensive as
18. Taichung

II. RADICAL IDENTIFICATION.

Provide the Pīnyīn for each of the following characters and put the radical component each set has in common in the parentheses to the right. [Hint: Refer to the Radicals section (pp. 1-10).]

暖 _____	春 _____	東 (东) _____	(_____)
鞋 _____	塊 (块) _____	熱 (热) _____	(_____)
床 _____	葉 (叶) _____	東 (东) _____	(_____)
國 (国) _____	圖 (图) _____	園 (园) _____	(_____)

III. MATCHING.

First, draw a line connecting the Pīnyīn to its traditional character. Then, connect the traditional character to its simplified counterpart. Finally, draw a line connecting the simplified character to its English meaning.

<u>Pīnyīn</u>	<u>Traditional</u>	<u>Simplified</u>	<u>English</u>
gāng	悶	叶	to make an appt.
liáng	葉	刚	strait; bay
mēn	約	约	just now
rè	園	闷	garden
wān	灣	园	image
xiàng	像	凉	stuffy
yè	涼	热	cool
yuán	熱	湾	leaf
yuē	剛	像	hot

IV. PHONOLOGICAL DISTINCTION.

Provide the full Pīnyīn for each of the following characters and then put the basic homonym (initial + final, but no tone) each set shares in the parentheses to the right.

工	_____	公	_____	共	_____	(_____)	
二	_____	而	_____	兒 (儿)	_____	(_____)	
也	_____	夜	_____	業 (业)	_____	(_____)	
出	_____	楚	_____	除 (除)	_____	(_____)	
付	_____	服	_____	復 (复)	_____	(_____)	
冬	_____	東 (东)	_____	懂 (懂)	_____	(_____)	
玩	_____	晚 (晚)	_____	灣 (湾)	_____	(_____)	

Dialogue I

寒		hán (†) cold	寒	寒				
		寒						
寒	宀	宁	宇	审	宭	実	寒	

假		jià (831) vacation	假	假				
		假						
假	亻	亻	亻	仴	作	俏	俏	假

飛	飞	fēi (357) to fly	飛	飞	飛	飛		
		飛 飞			飞	飞		
飛	乁	飞	飞	飛	飛	飛		
飞	乁	飞						

機	机	jī (125) machine	機	機				
see page 144		機 机	机	机				
機	木	樴	機					
机	木	机						

機   機   機

票		piào (†) ticket	票	票			
		票					
票	西	票					

場	场	chǎng (364) field	場	場			
		場	场	場	场		
場	土	圹	坍	場			
场	土	圬	场	场			

汽		qì (507) steam; gas	汽	汽			
		汽					
汽	氵	汽					

車	车	chē (178) car; vehicle	車	車			
		車	车	車	车		
車	車						
车	车						

場　　　場　　　場

或		huò (331) or	或	或			
		或					
或	一	豆	豆	或			

者		zhě (258) P	者	者			
		者 者					
者	土	尹	者				

地		dì / de (16) ground; P	地	地			
		地					
地	土	地					

鐵	铁	tiě (439) iron	鐵	铁			
see page 144		鐵 铁			铁	铁	
鐵	金	鉎	鋯	鐟	鐵		
铁	钅	钅	铁				

走		zǒu (104) to walk	走	走			
		走					
走	土	走					

| 站 | | zhàn (338) to stand; station | 站 | 站 | | | |
| 立 | 站 | 站 | | | | | |

綠	绿	lù (851) green	綠	绿	綠	綠	
					绿	绿	
綠	糸	綠					
绿	纟	绿					

線	线	xiàn (263) line; route	線	线	線	線	
			線	线	线	线	
線	糸	絈	線				
线	纟	线					

| 藍 | 蓝 | lán (†) blue | 藍 | 藍 | 藍 | 藍 | |
| | | | 藍 | 蓝 | 藍 | 藍 | |
see page 144

藍	艹	艹	艼	苦	莗	茛	藍	藍	蓝	藍	藍
蓝	艹	艹	艻	茊	苳	荶	蓝	蓝			

| 麻 | | má (†) hemp | 麻 | 麻 | | | |
| 麻 | 广 | 床 | 麻 | | | | |

煩	烦	fán (†) to trouble	煩	烦			
煩	火	煩					
烦	火	烦					

| 租 | | zū (†) to rent | 租 | 租 | | | |
| 租 | 禾 | 租 | | | | | |

送	送	sòng (469) to deliver; to send off	送	送			
送	丶	丷	关	送			
送	丶	丷	关	送			

麻   麻   麻

Dialogue II

過	过	guò (38) to pass			過	過			
		過	过		过	过			
過	冂	冂	叧	咼	咼	過			
过	寸	过							

讓	让	ràng (379) to let; to allow			讓	讓			
see page 144		讓	让		让	让			
讓	言	言	計	詾	諽	讓			
让	讠	让							

花	花	huā (240) flower; to spend			花	花			
		花	花		花	花			
花	艹	花							
花	艹	花							

每		měi (306) every; each			每	每			
		每							
每	⺈	每							

速	速	sù (503) speed		速	速			
		速	速		速	速		
速	一	亓	申	車	束	速		
速	一	亓	申	束	束	速		

路		lù (165) road; way		路	路			
		路						
路	足	路						

緊	緊	jǐn (412) tense; tight		緊	緊			
		系	緊		緊	緊		
緊	臣	臤	緊					
緊	丨	収	緊					

自		zì (63) self; from		自	自			
		自						
自	自							

緊   緊   緊

		jǐ (130)		己	己			
己		self						
		己						
己	己							

己
jǐ
'self'

巳
yǐ
'already'

巳
sì
'a period of time'
(9-11 am)

	1	2	3	4	5	6	7	8	9	10	11	12
1												
2												
3												
4												
5												
6												
7												
8												
9												
10												
11												
12												
	1	2	3	4	5	6	7	8	9	10	11	12

Fun With Characters

I. SEEK AND FIND.

Hidden in the box below are some words and phrases from the text. See how many you can find and circle them. Phrases can go horizontally left to right (→), vertically top to bottom (↓), or diagonally upper left to lower right (↘) or lower left to upper right (↗).

火	出	程	開	車	開	得	很	快
或	租	地	者	了	機	思	四	時
貨	汽	飛	煩	場	意	一	已	以
過	車	麻	機	好	號	合	和	寒
然	太	馬	不	票	給	台	加	假
高	貴	真	方	用	你	下	拿	你
速	機	票	便	宜	客	買	會	回
公	共	汽	車	到	課	氣	了	家
路	六	你	知	道	怎	麼	走	嗎

II. RADICAL IDENTIFICATION.

Provide the Pīnyīn for each of the following characters and put the radical component each set has in common in the parentheses to the right. [Hint: Refer to the Radicals section (pp. 1-10).]

做 _____   作 _____   坐 _____   (_____)

我 _____   找 _____   或 _____   (_____)

酒 _____   漂 _____   沒 (沒) _____   (_____)

因 _____   回 _____   圖 (图) _____   (_____)

覺 (觉) _____   視 (视) _____   現 (现) _____   (_____)

III. MATCHING.

First, draw a line connecting the Pīnyīn to its traditional character. Then, connect the traditional character to its simplified counterpart. Finally, draw a line connecting the simplified character to its English meaning.

Pīnyīn	Traditional	Simplified	English
chǎng	讓	线	blue
chē	鐵	绿	green
fán	藍	速	tense; tight
fēi	機	送	to allow
guò	線	让	to deliver
huā	綠	铁	to fly
jī	緊	蓝	to pass
jǐn	場	紧	to trouble
lán	過	机	car
lǜ	煩	花	field
ràng	速	过	flower
sòng	送	飞	iron
sù	飛	烦	line
tiě	花	车	machine
xiàn	車	场	speed

IV. FILL IN THE SQUARES.

Fill in each of the empty squares below with one character each that contains the radical component provided.

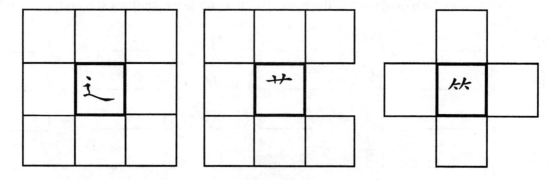

INDEXES

Enlarged Characters for Easier Viewing

Lesson 1	Lesson 1	Lesson 2
麼	學	醫
see page 17	*see page 20*	*see page 33*
me	xué	yī

Lesson 3	Lesson 3	Lesson 3
歡	鐘	識
see page 41	*see page 42*	*see page 47*
huān	zhōng	shí

Lesson 5	Lesson 6	Lesson 6
圖	會	幇
see page 69	*see page 74*	*see page 79*
tú	huì	bāng

Lesson 6	Lesson 7	Lesson 7
練	難	裏
see page 79	*see page 84*	*see page 85*
liàn	nán	lǐ

Lesson 8	Lesson 8	Lesson 8
邊	餐	廳
see page 92	*see page 95*	*see page 95*
biān	cān	tīng

Lesson 9	Lesson 9	Lesson 9
襯	顏	褲
see page 107	*see page 107*	*see page 109*
chèn	yán	kù

Lesson 10	Lesson 10	Lesson 11
糟	灣	機
see page 121	*see page 124*	*see page 127*
zāo	wān	jī

Lesson 11	Lesson 11	Lesson 11
鐵	藍	讓
see page 129	*see page 130*	*see page 133*
tiě	lán	ràng

Integrated Chinese I (Part 1) — Character Index
Chronological by Lesson
(Lessons 1-11, including Radicals and Numerals)

*	=	bound form
M	=	Measure word
P	=	Particle
QP	=	Question Particle

Radicals

人(亻)	rén	man; person
刀(刂)	dāo	knife
力	lì	power
又	yòu	right hand; again
口	kǒu	mouth
囗	wéi	enclose
土	tǔ	earth
夕	xī	sunset
大	dà	big; large
女	nǚ	female; woman
子	zǐ	son; child
寸	cùn	inch
小	xiǎo	little; small
工	gōng	labor; work; craft
幺	yāo	tiny; small
弓	gōng	bow
心(忄)	xīn	heart
戈	gē	dagger-axe
手(扌)	shǒu	hand
日	rì	sun
月	yuè	moon
木	mù	wood
水(氵)	shuǐ	water
火(灬)	huǒ	fire
田	tián	field
目	mù	eye
示(礻)	shì	to show
糸/纟	mì	fine silk
耳	ěr	ear
衣(衤)	yī	clothing
言/讠	yán	word
貝/贝	bèi	cowry shell
走	zǒu	to walk
足	zú	foot
金	jīn	metal; gold
門/门	mén	door; gate
隹	zhuī	short-tailed bird
雨	yǔ	rain
食	shí	to eat
馬/马	mǎ	horse

Numerals

一	yī	one
二	èr	two
三	sān	three
四	sì	four
五	wǔ	five
六	liù	six
七	qī	seven
八	bā	eight
九	jiǔ	nine
十	shí	ten

Lesson 1: Greetings				**Lesson 2**		
先		xiān	first	那／那		nà / nèi	that
生		shēng	born	張／张		zhāng	M
你		nǐ	you	照		zhào	shine
好		hǎo/hào	good; fine; O.K.	片		piàn	*film; slice
小		xiǎo	little; small	的		de	P
姐		jiě	older sister	這／这		zhè(i)	this
王		wáng	(a surname); king	爸		bà	dad
李		lǐ	(a surname); plum	媽／妈		mā	mom
請／请		qǐng	please; invite	個／个		gè	M (general)
問／问		wèn	ask	男		nán	male
您		nín	you (polite)	孩		hái	child
貴／贵		guì	honorable	子		zǐ	son
姓		xìng	surname	誰／谁		shéi	who
我		wǒ	I; me	他		tā	he
呢		ne	QP	弟		dì	younger brother
叫		jiào	call	女		nǚ	female
什(甚)		shén	*what	妹		mèi	younger sister
麼／么		me	*QP	她		tā	she
名		míng	name	兒／儿		ér	son; child
字		zì	character	有		yǒu	have; there is/are
朋		péng	friend	沒(没)		méi	(have) not
友		yǒu	friend	高		gāo	tall
是		shì	be	家		jiā	family; home
老		lǎo	old	幾／几		jǐ	QP; how many
師／师		shī	teacher	哥		gē	older brother
嗎／吗		ma	QP	兩／两		liǎng	two; a couple of
不		bù	not; no	和		hé (huo)	and / *warm
學／学		xué	study	做		zuò	do
也		yě	also; too	英／英		yīng	*England
中		zhōng	center; middle	文		wén	script
國／国		guó	country	律		lù	law; rule
人		rén	man; person	都／都		dōu	all; both
美		měi	beautiful	醫／医		yī	medicine; doctor

Lesson 3

月		yuè	moon; month
號／号		hào	number
星		xīng	star
期		qī	period (of time)
天		tiān	sky; day
日		rì	day
今		jīn	today; now
年		nián	year
多		duō	many
大		dà	big
歲／岁		suì	age
吃		chī	eat
晚／晚		wǎn	evening; late
飯／饭		fàn	meal
怎		zěn	*how
樣／样		yàng	kind
太		tài	too; extremely
了		le	P
謝／谢		xiè	thank
喜		xǐ	*like; happy
歡／欢		huān	joyful
還／还		hái	still; yet
可		kě	but
們／们		men	*(plural suffix)
點／点		diǎn	dot; o'clock
鐘／钟		zhōng	clock
半		bàn	half
上		shàng	above; top
見／见		jiàn	see
再		zài	again
白		bái	white
現／现		xiàn	now
在		zài	at; in; on
刻		kè	quarter (hour)
明		míng	bright

忙		máng	busy
很		hěn	very
事		shì	affair; matter
為／为		wèi/wéi	for
因		yīn	because
同		tóng	same
認／认		rèn	recognize
識／识		shí	recognize

Lesson 4

週／周		zhōu	week
末		mò	end
打		dǎ	hit; strike
球		qiú	ball
看		kàn	see; look
電／电		diàn	electric
視／视		shì	view
唱		chàng	sing
歌		gē	song
跳		tiào	jump
舞		wǔ	dance
聽／听		tīng	listen
音		yīn	sound; music
樂／乐		yuè	music
對／对		duì	correct; toward
時／时		shí	time
候		hòu	wait
書／书		shū	book
影		yǐng	shadow
常		cháng	often
去		qù	go
外		wài	outside
客		kè	guest
昨		zuó	yesterday
所(所)		suǒ	*so; place
以		yǐ	with

久		jiǔ	long time
錯	／錯	cuò	wrong; error
想		xiǎng	think
覺	／觉	jiào/jué	sleep; feel; reckon
得		dé / de	obtain; get; P
意		yì	meaning
思		sī	think
只		zhǐ	only
睡		shuì	sleep
算		suàn	calculate; figure
找		zhǎo	look for; seek
別	／别	bié	other

要		yào	want
杯		bēi	cup; glass
起		qǐ	rise
給	／给	gěi	give
水		shuǐ	water
玩		wán	play; visit
圖	／图	tú	drawing
館	／馆	guǎn	accomodations
瓶		píng	bottle
聊		liáo	chat
才		cái	not until; only
回		huí	return

Lesson 5

呀		ya	P
進	／进	jìn	enter
快		kuài	fast; quick
來	／来	lái	come
介		jiè	between
紹	／绍	shào	carry on
下		xià	below; under
興	／兴	xìng	mood; interest
漂		piào	*pretty
亮	／亮	liàng	bright
坐		zuò	sit
哪	／哪	nǎ / něi	which
		gōng	labor; work; craft
工		zuò	work; do
作		xiào	school
校		hē	drink
喝		chá	tea
茶	／茶	kā	*coffee
咖		fēi	*coffee
啡		pí	*beer
啤		jiǔ	wine
酒		ba	P
吧			

Lesson 6

話	／话	huà	speech
喂		wèi	Hello!; Hey!
就		jiù	just
位		wèi	M (polite)
午		wǔ	noon
間	／间	jiān	M (for rooms)
題	／题	tí	topic; question
開	／开	kāi	open
會	／会	huì	meet
節	／节	jié	M (for classes)
課	／课	kè	class; lesson
級	／级	jí	grade; level
考		kǎo	test
試	／试	shì	try
後	／后	hòu	after
空		kòng	free time
方		fāng	square; side
便		biàn	convenient
到		dào	go to; arrive
辦	／办	bàn	manage
公		gōng	public
室		shì	room

行		xíng/háng	all right; O.K. / firm
等		děng	wait
氣／气		qì	air
幫／帮		bāng	help
練／练		liàn	drill
習／习		xí	practice
說／说		shuō	speak
啊／啊		a	P
但		dàn	but
知		zhī	know
道／道		dào	road; way

Lesson 7

跟		gēn	with; and
助		zhù	assist
復／复		fù	duplicate
寫／写		xiě	write
慢		màn	slow
教(敎)		jiāo	teach
筆／笔		bǐ	pen
難／难		nán	difficult; hard
裏｜裡｜里		lǐ	inside
第		dì	(ordinal prefix)
預／预		yù	prepare
語／语		yǔ	language
法		fǎ	method; way
容		róng	hold; contain; allow
易		yì	easy
懂／懂		dǒng	understand
詞／词		cí	word
漢／汉		hàn	Chinese
平		píng	level; even
早		zǎo	early
夜		yè	night
功		gōng	skill
真(眞)		zhēn	true; real

始		shǐ	begin
唸／念		niàn	read
錄／录		lù	record
帥／帅		shuài	handsome; smart

Lesson 8

篇		piān	M (for articles)
記／记		jì	record
床(牀)		chuáng	bed
洗		xǐ	wash
澡		zǎo	bath
邊／边		biān	side
教(敎)		jiào	teaching
發／发		fā	emit; issue
新		xīn	new
腦／脑		nǎo	brain
餐		cān	meal
廳／厅		tīng	hall
報／报		bào	newspaper
宿		sù	stay
舍		shè	house
正		zhèng	just; straight
前		qián	front; before
告		gào	tell; inform
訴／诉		sù	tell; relate
已		yǐ	already
經／经		jīng	pass through
封		fēng	M (for letters)
信		xìn	letter
最		zuì	most
近／近		jìn	near
除／除		chú	except
專／专		zhuān	special
業／业		yè	occupation
慣／惯		guàn	be used to
清		qíng	clear; clean

楚		chǔ	clear; neat
步		bù	step
希		xī	hope
望／望		wàng	hope; wish
能		néng	be able
用		yòng	use
笑		xiào	laugh
祝		zhù	wish

Lesson 9

買／买		mǎi	buy
東／东		dōng	east
西		xī	west
售		shòu	sell
貨／货		huò	merchandise
員／员		yuán	personnel
衣		yī	clothing
服		fú	clothing
件		jiàn	M (for items)
襯／衬		chèn	lining
衫		shān	shirt
顏／颜		yán	face; countenance
色		sè	color
黄(黃)		huáng	yellow
紅／红		hóng	red
穿		chuān	wear
條／条		tiáo	M (for long objects)
褲／裤		kù	pants
宜		yí	suitable
付		fù	pay
錢／钱		qián	money
共		gòng	altogether
少		shǎo	few
塊／块		kuài	piece; dollar
毛		máo	hair; dime
分		fēn	penny; minute

百		bǎi	hundred
雙／双		shuāng	pair
鞋		xié	shoes
換／换		huàn	change
黑		hēi	black
雖／虽		suī	though; while
然		rán	like that; so
合		hé	suit; agree
適／适		shì	suit; fit

Lesson 10

比		bǐ	compare
雨		yǔ	rain
更		gèng	even more
而		ér	and; in addition
且		qiě	for the time being
暖		nuǎn	warm
約／约		yuē	make an appointment
園／园		yuán	garden
葉／叶		yè	leaf
像		xiàng	image
海		hǎi	sea
糟		zāo	messy
糕		gāo	cake
又		yòu	again
剛／刚		gāng	just now
出		chū	go out
熱／热		rè	hot
舒		shū	stretch
夏		xià	summer
涼／凉		liáng	cool
春		chūn	spring
冬		dōng	winter
冷		lěng	cold
悶／闷		mēn	stuffy
次		cì	M (for occurance)

秋	qiū	autumn; fall
台(臺)	tái	platform
北	běi	north
灣／湾	wān	strait; bay

Lesson 11

寒		hán	cold
假		jià	vacation
飛／飞		fēi	fly
機／机		jī	machine
票		piào	ticket
場／场		chǎng	field
汽		qì	steam
車／车		chē	car
或		huò	or
者		zhě	(a suffix)
地		dì	earth
鐵／铁		tiě	iron

走		zǒu	walk
站		zhàn	stand; station
綠／绿		lù	green
線／线		xiàn	line
藍／蓝		lán	blue
麻		má	hemp; numb
煩／烦		fán	bother
租		zū	rent
送／送		sòng	deliver
過／过		guò	pass
讓／让		ràng	let
花／花		huā	spend
每		měi	every
速／速		sù	speed
路		lù	road; way
緊／紧		jǐn	tight
自		zì	self
己		jǐ	oneself

Integrated Chinese I (Part 1) — Character Index
Alphabetical by Pīnyīn

* =	bound form	
M =	Measure word	
P =	Particle	
QP =	Question Particle	

A

啊／啊	a	P	6.2

B

八	bā	eight	Num
爸	bà	dad	2.1
吧	ba	P	5.1
白	bái	white	3.1
百	bǎi	hundred	9.1
半	bàn	half	3.1
辦／办	bàn	manage	6.1
幫／帮	bāng	help	6.2
報／报	bào	newspaper	8.1
杯	bēi	cup; glass	5.1
北	běi	north	10.2
貝／贝	bèi	cowry shell	Rad
筆／笔	bǐ	pen	7.1
比	bǐ	compare	10.1
邊／边	biān	side	8.1
便	biàn	convenient	6.1
別／别	bié	other	4.2
不	bù	not; no	1.3
步	bù	step	8.2

C

才	cái	not until; only	5.2
餐	cān	meal	8.1
茶／茶	chá	tea	5.1
常	cháng	often	4.1
場／场	chǎng	field	11.1
唱	chàng	sing	4.1

車／车	chē	car	11.1
襯／衬	chèn	lining	9.1
吃	chī	eat	3.1
出	chū	go out	10.2
除／除	chú	except	8.2
楚	chǔ	clear; neat	8.2
穿	chuān	wear	9.1
床(牀)	chuáng	bed	8.1
春	chūn	spring	10.2
詞／词	cí	word	7.1
次	cì	M (for occurances)	10.2
寸	cùn	inch	Rad
錯／错	cuò	wrong; error	4.2

D

打	dǎ	hit; strike	4.1
大	dà	big	Rad, 3.1
但	dàn	but	6.2
刀(刂)	dāo	knife	Rad
到	dào	arrive	6.1
道／道	dào	road; way	6.2
得	dé	obtain; get	4.2
的	de	P	2.1
得	děi	must; have to	6.1
地	de	P	11.1
等	děng	wait	6.1
弟	dì	younger brother	2.1
第	dì	(ordinal prefix)	7.1
地	dì	earth	11.1
點／点	diǎn	dot; o'clock	3.1
電／电	diàn	electric	4.1

R			
然	rán	like that; so	9.2
讓／让	ràng	let; allow	11.2
熱／热	rè	hot	10.2
人(亻)	rén	man; person	Rad, 1.3
認／认	rèn	to recognize	3.2
日	rì	sun; day	Rad, 3.1
容	róng	hold; contain	7.1
S			
三	sān	three	Num
色	sè	color	9.1
衫	shān	shirt	9.1
上	shàng	above; on top	3.1
少	shǎo	few	9.1
紹／绍	shào	carry on	5.1
舍	shè	house	8.1
誰／谁	shéi	who	2.1
什(甚)	shén	*what	1.2
生	shēng	be born	1.1
師／师	shī	teacher	1.3
食	shí	to eat	Rad
十	shí	ten	Num
識／识	shí	to recognize	3.2
時／时	shí	time	4.1
始	shǐ	begin	7.2
示(礻)	shì	to show	Rad
是	shì	be	1.3
事	shì	matter; affair	3.2
視／视	shì	view	4.1
室	shì	room	6.1
試／试	shì	try	6.1
適／适	shì	suit; fit	9.2
手(扌)	shǒu	hand	Rad
售	shòu	sell	9.1

書／书	shū	book	4.1
舒	shū	stretch	10.2
帥／帅	shuài	handsome	7.2
雙／双	shuāng	pair	9.2
水(氵)	shuǐ	water	Rad, 5.1
睡	shuì	sleep	4.2
說／说	shuō	speak	6.2
思	sī	think	4.2
四	sì	four	Num
送／送	sòng	deliver	11.1
宿	sù	stay	8.1
訴／诉	sù	tell; relate	8.1
速／速	sù	speed	11.2
算	suàn	calculate; figure	4.2
雖／虽	suī	though; while	9.2
歲／岁	suì	age	3.1
所(所)	suǒ	*so; place	4.1
T			
他	tā	he	2.1
她	tā	she	2.1
台(臺)	tái	platform	10.2
太	tài	too; extremely	3.1
題／题	tí	topic; question	6.1
天	tiān	sky; day	3.1
田	tián	(a surname); field	Rad
條／条	tiáo	M (for long objects)	9.1
跳	tiào	jump	4.1
聽／听	tīng	listen	4.1
廳／厅	tīng	hall	8.1
同	tóng	same	3.2
圖／图	tú	drawing	5.2
土	tǔ	earth	Rad

友	yǒu	friend	1.2
有	yǒu	have; there is/are	2.1
又	yòu	again	Rad, 10.2
語／语	yǔ	language	7.1
雨	yǔ	rain	Rad, 10.1
預／预	yù	prepare	7.1
員／员	yuán	personnel	9.1
園／园	yuán	garden	10.1
約／约	yuē	make an appoint.	10.1
月	yuè	moon; month	Rad, 3.1
樂／乐	yuè	music	4.1

Z

再	zài	again	3.1
在	zài	at; in; on	3.2
糟	zāo	messy	10.2
早	zǎo	early	7.2
澡	zǎo	bath	8.1
怎	zěn	*how	3.1
站	zhàn	stand; station	11.1
張／张	zhāng	M; (a surname)	2.1
找	zhǎo	look for; seek	4.2
照	zhào	shine	2.1
者	zhě	(a suffix)	11.1

這／这	zhè(i)	this	2.1
真(眞)	zhēn	true; real	7.2
正	zhèng	just; straight	8.1
知	zhī	know	6.2
只	zhǐ	only	4.2
中	zhōng	center; middle	1.3
鐘／钟	zhōng	clock	3.1
週／周	zhōu	week	4.1
助	zhù	assist	7.1
祝	zhù	wish	8.2
專／专	zhuān	special	8.2
佳	zhuī	short-tailed bird	Rad
子	zǐ	son	Rad, 2.1
字	zì	character	1.2
自	zì	self	11.2
走	zǒu	walk	Rad, 11.1
租	zū	rent	11.1
足	zú	foot	Rad
最	zuì	most	8.2
昨	zuó	yesterday	4.1
做	zuò	do	2.2
坐	zuò	sit	5.1
作	zuò	work; do	5.1

Integrated Chinese I (Part 1) — Traditional Character Index
Arranged by Number of Strokes

*	=	bound form
M	=	Measure word
P	=	Particle
QP	=	Question Particle

1

一	yī	one	Num

2

八	bā	eight	Num
刀(刂)	dāo	knife	Rad
二	èr	two	Num
九	jiǔ	nine	Num
了	le	P	3.1
力	lì	power; strength	Rad
七	qī	seven	Num
人(亻)	rén	man; person	Rad, 1.2
十	shí	ten	Num
又	yòu	again	Rad, 10.2

3

才	cái	not until; only	5.2
寸	cùn	inch	Rad
大	dà	big	Rad, 3.1
工	gōng	craft; work	Rad, 5.1
弓	gōng	bow	Rad
己	jǐ	oneself	11.2
久	jiǔ	long time	4.2
口	kǒu	mouth	Rad
女	nǚ	woman; female	Rad, 2.1
三	sān	three	Num
上	shàng	above; on top	3.1
土	tǔ	earth	Rad
口	wéi	enclose	Rad
夕	xī	sunset	Rad

下	xià	below; under	5.1
小	xiǎo	little; small	Rad, 1.1
幺	yāo	tiny; small	Rad
也	yě	also	1.2
已	yǐ	already	8.1
子	zǐ	son	Rad, 2.1

4

比	bǐ	compare	10.1
不	bù	not; no	1.2
方	fāng	square; side	6.1
分	fēn	penny; minute	9.1
戈	gē	dagger-axe	Rad
公	gōng	public	6.1
火(灬)	huǒ	fire	Rad
介	jiè	between	5.1
今	jīn	today; now	3.1
六	liù	six	Num
毛	máo	hair; dime	9.1
木	mù	wood	Rad
片	piàn	slice; *film	2.1
日	rì	sun; day	Rad, 3.1
少	shǎo	few	9.1
什(甚)	shén	*what	1.1
手	shǒu	hand	Rad
水(氵)	shuǐ	water	Rad, 5.1
太	tài	too; extremely	3.1
天	tiān	sky; day	3.1
王	wáng	(a surname); king	1.1
文	wén	script	2.2
五	wǔ	five	Num

午	wǔ	noon	6.1
心/忄	xīn	heart	Rad
以	yǐ	with	4.1
友	yǒu	friend	1.1
月	yuè	moon; month	Rad, 3.1
中	zhōng	center; middle	1.2

5

白	bái	white	3.1
半	bàn	half	3.1
北	běi	north	10.2
出	chū	go out	10.2
打	dǎ	hit; strike	4.1
冬	dōng	winter	10.2
付	fù	pay	9.1
功	gōng	skill	7.2
叫	jiào	call	1.1
可	kě	but	3.1
末	mò	end	4.1
目	mù	eye	Rad
平	píng	level; even	7.2
且	qiě	for the time being	10.1
去	qù	go	4.1
生	shēng	be born	1.1
示(礻)	shì	to show	Rad
四	sì	four	Num
他	tā	he	2.1
台(臺)	tái	platform	10.2
田	tián	(a surname); field	Rad
外	wài	outside	4.1
用	yòng	use	8.2
正	zhèng	just; straight	8.1
只	zhǐ	only	4.2

6

百	bǎi	hundred	9.1
吃	chī	eat	3.1
次	cì	M (for occurances)	10.2
地	dì / de	earth	11.1
多	duō	many	3.1
而	ér	and	10.1
耳	ěr	ear	Rad
共	gòng	altogether	9.1
好	hǎo	fine; good; OK	1.1
好	hào	like; be fond of	4.1
合	hé	suit; agree	9.2
回	huí	return	5.2
件	jiàn	M (for items)	9.1
考	kǎo	test	6.1
老	lǎo	old	1.2
忙	máng	busy	3.2
糸	mì	fine silk	Rad
名	míng	name	1.1
年	nián	year	3.1
色	sè	color	9.1
她	tā	she	2.1
同	tóng	same	3.2
西	xī	west	9.1
先	xiān	first	1.1
行	xíng	all right; O.K.	6.1
衣(礻)	yī	clothing	Rad, 9.1
因	yīn	because	3.2
有	yǒu	have; there is/are	2.1
再	zài	again	3.1
在	zài	at; in; on	3.2
早	zǎo	early	7.2
字	zì	character	1.1
自	zì	self	11.2

7

吧	ba	P	5.1
貝／贝	bèi	cowry shell	Rad
別／别	bié	other	4.2
步	bù	step	8.2
車／车	chē	car	11.1
床(牀)	chuáng	bed	8.1
但	dàn	but	6.2
弟	dì	younger brother	2.1
告	gào	tell; inform	8.1
更	gèng	even more	10.1
見／见	jiàn	see	3.1
快	kuài	fast; quick	5.1
冷	lěng	cold	10.2
李	lǐ	(a surname); plum	1.1
没(沒)	méi	(have) not	2.1
每	měi	every; each	11.2
那／那	nà / nèi	that	2.1
男	nán	male	2.1
你	nǐ	you	1.1
汽	qì	steam	11.1
位	wèi	M (polite)	6.1
我	wǒ	I; me	1.1
希	xī	hope	8.2
言	yán	word	Rad
找	zhǎo	look for; seek	4.2
助	zhù	assist	7.1
走	zǒu	walk	Rad, 11.1
足	zú	foot	Rad
坐	zuò	sit	5.1
作	zuò	work; do	5.1

8

爸	bà	dad	2.1
杯	bēi	cup; glass	5.1
到	dào	arrive	6.1
的	de	P	2.1
東／东	dōng	east	9.1
兒／儿	ér	son; child	2.1
法	fǎ	method; way	7.1
服	fú	clothing	9.1
和	hé/huo	and/*warm	2.2/10.1
花／花	huā	spend	11.2
或	huò	or	11.1
金	jīn	(a surname); gold	Rad
門／门	mén	door; gate	Rad
衫	shān	shirt	9.1
舍	shè	house	8.1
始	shǐ	begin	7.2
事	shì	matter; affair	3.2
所(所)	suǒ	*so; place	4.1
姓	xìng	surname	1.1
夜	yè	night	7.2
宜	yí	suitable	9.1
易	yì	easy	7.1
雨	yǔ	rain	Rad, 10.1
隹	zhuī	short-tailed bird	Rad

9

便	biàn	convenient	6.1
穿	chuān	wear	9.1
春	chūn	spring	10.2
飛／飞	fēi	fly	11.1
封	fēng	M (for letters)	8.2
孩	hái	child	2.1
很	hěn	very	3.2

啡	fēi	*coffee	5.1
國／国	guó	country	1.2
黃(黄)	huáng	yellow	9.1
貨／货	huò	merchandise	9.1
假	jià	vacation	11.1
教／教	jiāo	teach	7.1
涼／凉	liáng	cool	10.2
聊	liáo	chat	5.2
麻	má	hemp; numb	11.1
唸／念	niàn	read	7.2
您	nín	you (polite)	1.1
啤	pí	*beer	5.1
票	piào	ticket	11.1
清	qīng	clear; clean	8.2
球	qiú	ball	4.1
紹／绍	shào	carry on	5.1
視／视	shì	view	4.1
售	shòu	sell	9.1
宿	sù	stay	8.1
速／速	sù	speed	11.2
條／条	tiáo	M (for long objects)	9.1
望／望	wàng	hope; wish	8.2
問／问	wèn	ask	1.1
習／习	xí	study; review	6.2
現／现	xiàn	present	3.2
張／张	zhāng	M; (a surname)	2.1
這／这	zhè(i)	this	2.1
專／专	zhuān	special	8.2
做	zuò	do	2.2

12

報／报	bào	newspaper	8.1
筆／笔	bǐ	pen	7.1
場／场	chǎng	field	11.1
詞／词	cí	word	7.1
等	děng	wait	6.1
發／发	fā	emit; issue	8.1
飯／饭	fàn	meal	3.1
復／复	fù	duplicate	7.1
給／给	gěi	give	5.1
貴／贵	guì	honorable	1.1
喝	hē	drink	5.1
黑	hēi	black	9.2
換／换	huàn	change	9.2
幾／几	jǐ	QP; how many	2.2
間／间	jiān	M (for rooms)	6.1
進／进	jìn	enter	5.1
就	jiù	just	6.1
開／开	kāi	open	6.1
裡｜裏｜里	lǐ	inside	7.1
買／买	mǎi	buy	9.1
悶／闷	mēn	stuffy	10.2
期	qī	period (of time)	3.1
然	rán	like that; so	9.2
試／试	shì	try	6.1
舒	shū	stretch	10.2
訴／诉	sù	tell; relate	8.1
晚／晚	wǎn	evening; late	3.1
喂	wèi	Hello!; Hey!	6.1
喜	xǐ	like; happy	3.1
葉／叶	yè	leaf	10.1
園／园	yuán	garden	10.1
週／周	zhōu	week	4.1
最	zuì	most	8.2

13				
楚		chǔ	clear; neat	8.2
道／道		dào	road; way	6.2
電／电		diàn	electric	4.1
煩／烦		fán	bother	11.1
跟		gēn	with; and	7.1
過／过		guò	pass	11.2
號／号		hào	number	3.1
話／话		huà	speech	6.1
會／会		huì	meet	6.1
塊／块		kuài	piece; dollar	9.1
節／节		jié	M (for classes)	6.1
經／经		jīng	pass through	8.1
裏／裡／里		lǐ	inside	7.1
路		lù	road; way	11.2
媽／妈		mā	mom	2.1
嗎／吗		ma	QP	1.2
腦／脑		nǎo	brain	8.1
暖		nuǎn	warm	10.1
睡		shuì	sleep	4.2
歲／岁		suì	age	3.1
跳		tiào	jump	4.1
想		xiǎng	think	4.2
新		xīn	new	8.1
業／业		yè	occupation	8.2
意		yì	meaning	4.2
預／预		yù	prepare	7.1
照		zhào	shine	2.1

14				
對／对		duì	correct; toward	4.1
歌		gē	song	4.1
慣／惯		guàn	be used to	8.2
漢／汉		hàn	Chinese	7.1

緊／紧		jǐn	tight	11.2
綠／绿		lù	green	11.1
慢		màn	slow	7.1
麼／么		me	*QP	1.1
漂		piào	*pretty	5.1
認／认		rèn	to recognize	3.2
說／说		shuō	speak	6.2
算		suàn	calculate; figure	4.2
圖／图		tú	drawing	5.2
舞		wǔ	dance	4.1
像		xiàng	image	10.1
寫／写		xiě	write	7.1
語／语		yǔ	language	7.1

15				
課／课		kè	class; lesson	6.1
褲／裤		kù	pants	9.1
樂／乐		lè	happy	5.1 (4.1)
練／练		liàn	practice; drill	6.2
篇		piān	M (for articles)	8.1
請／请		qǐng	please; invite	1.1
熱／热		rè	hot	10.2
誰／谁		shéi	who	2.1
適／适		shì	suit; fit	9.2
線／线		xiàn	line	11.1
鞋		xié	shoes	9.2
樣／样		yàng	kind	3.1
影		yǐng	shadow	4.1
樂／乐		yuè	music	4.1

16				
辦／办		bàn	manage	6.1
餐		cān	meal	8.1
錯／错		cuò	wrong; error	4.2

懂／懂	dǒng	understand	7.1
糕	gāo	cake	10.2
館／馆	guǎn	accommodations	5.2
機／机	jī	machine	11.1
錄／录	lù	record	7.2
錢／钱	qián	money	9.1
興／兴	xìng	mood; interest	5.1
學／学	xué	study	1.2
澡	zǎo	bath	8.1

17

幫／帮	bāng	help	6.2
點／点	diǎn	dot; o'clock	3.1
雖／虽	suī	though; while	9.2
謝／谢	xiè	thank	3.1
糟	zāo	messy	10.2

18

藍／蓝	lán	blue	11.1
雙／双	shuāng	pair	9.2
題／题	tí	topic; question	6.1
顏／颜	yán	face; countenance	9.1
醫／医	yī	doctor; medicine	2.2

19

邊／边	biān	side	8.1
難／难	nán	difficult; hard	7.1
識／识	shí	to recognize	3.2

20

覺／觉	jiào	sleep	4.2
覺／觉	jué	feel; reckon	4.2
鐘／钟	zhōng	clock	3.1

21

| 襯／衬 | chèn | lining | 9.1 |
| 鐵／铁 | tiě | iron | 11.1 |

22

| 歡／欢 | huān | joyful | 3.1 |
| 聽／听 | tīng | listen | 4.1 |

24

| 讓／让 | ràng | let; allow | 11.2 |

25

| 廳／厅 | tīng | hall | 8.1 |
| 灣／湾 | wān | strait; bay | 10.2 |

Integrated Chinese I, Part 1 — Simplified Character Index
Arranged by Number of Strokes

*	=	bound form
M	=	Measure word
P	=	Particle
QP	=	Question Particle

1

一	yī	one	Num

2

八	bā	eight	Num
刀(刂)	dāo	knife	Rad
儿／兒	ér	son; child	2.1
二	èr	two	Num
几／幾	jǐ	QP; how many	2.2
九	jiǔ	nine	Num
了	le	P	3.1
力	lì	power; strength	Rad
七	qī	seven	Num
人(亻)	rén	man; person	Rad, 1.2
十	shí	ten	Num
又	yòu	again	Rad, 10.2

3

才	cái	not until; only	5.2
寸	cùn	inch	Rad
大	dà	big	Rad, 3.1
飞／飛	fēi	fly	11.1
个／個	gè	M (general)	2.1
工	gōng	craft; work	Rad, 5.1
弓	gōng	bow	Rad
女	nǚ	woman; female	Rad, 2.1
己	jǐ	oneself	11.2
久	jiǔ	long time	4.2
口	kǒu	mouth	Rad
马／馬	mǎ	horse	Rad
么／麼	me	*QP	1.1
门／門	mén	door; gate	Rad
三	sān	three	Num
上	shàng	above; on top	3.1
土	tǔ	earth	Rad
口	wéi	enclose	Rad
夕	xī	sunset	Rad
习／習	xí	study; review	6.2
下	xià	below; under	5.1
小	xiǎo	little; small	Rad, 1.1
幺	yāo	tiny; small	Rad
也	yě	also	1.2
已	yǐ	already	8.1
子	zǐ	son	Rad, 2.1

4

办／辦	bàn	manage	6.1
贝／貝	bèi	cowry shell	Rad
比	bǐ	compare	10.1
不	bù	not; no	1.2
车／車	chē	car	11.1
方	fāng	square; side	6.1
分	fēn	penny; minute	9.1
戈	gē	dagger-axe	Rad
公	gōng	public	6.1
火(灬)	huǒ	fire	Rad
见／見	jiàn	see	3.1
介	jiè	between	5.1
今	jīn	today; now	3.1
开／開	kāi	open	6.1
六	liù	six	Num
毛	máo	hair; dime	9.1
木	mù	wood	Rad
片	piàn	slice; *film	2.1
气／氣	qì	air	6.1

而		ér	and	10.1
耳		ěr	ear	Rad
刚	/ 剛	gāng	just now	10.2
共		gòng	altogether	9.1
过	/ 過	guò	pass	11.2
好		hǎo	fine; good; OK	1.1
好		hào	like; be fond of	4.1
合		hé	suit; agree	9.2
红	/ 紅	hóng	red	9.1
后	/ 後	hòu	after	6.1
欢	/ 歡	huān	joyful	3.1
回		huí	return	5.2
会	/ 會	huì	meet	6.1
机	/ 機	jī	machine	11.1
级	/ 級	jí	grade; level	6.1
件		jiàn	M (for items)	9.1
考		kǎo	test	6.1
老		lǎo	old	1.2
妈	/ 媽	mā	mom	2.1
吗	/ 嗎	ma	QP	1.2
买	/ 買	mǎi	buy	9.1
忙		máng	busy	3.2
系	(纟)	mì	fine silk	Rad
名		míng	name	1.1
那	/ 那	nà / nèi	that	2.1
年		nián	year	3.1
色		sè	color	9.1
师	/ 師	shī	teacher	1.2
岁	/ 歲	suì	age	3.1
她		tā	she	2.1
同		tóng	same	3.2
问	/ 問	wèn	ask	1.1
西		xī	west	9.1
先		xiān	first	1.1
行		xíng	all right; O.K.	6.1
兴	/ 興	xìng	mood; interest	5.1

衣	(衤)	yī	clothing	Rad, 9.1
因		yīn	because	3.2
有		yǒu	have; there is/are	2.1
约	/ 約	yuē	make an appoint.	10.1
再		zài	again	3.1
在		zài	at; in; on	3.2
早		zǎo	early	7.2
字		zì	character	1.1
自		zì	self	11.2

7

吧		ba	P	5.1
报	/ 報	bào	newspaper	8.1
别	/ 別	bié	other	4.2
步		bù	step	8.2
床	/ 牀	chuáng	bed	8.1
词	/ 詞	cí	word	7.1
但		dàn	but	6.2
弟		dì	younger brother	2.1
饭	/ 飯	fàn	meal	3.1
告		gào	tell; inform	8.1
更		gèng	even more	10.1
花	/ 花	huā	spend	11.2
间	/ 間	jiān	M (for rooms)	6.1
进	/ 進	jìn	enter	5.1
快		kuài	fast; quick	5.1
块	/ 塊	kuài	piece; dollar	9.1
冷		lěng	cold	10.2
李		lǐ	(a surname); plum	1.1
里	裡 / 裏	lǐ	inside	7.1
没	(沒)	méi	(have) not	2.1
每		měi	every; each	11.2
闷	/ 悶	mēn	stuffy	10.2
男		nán	male	2.1
你		nǐ	you	1.1
汽		qì	steam	11.1

识 / 識	shí	to recognize	3.2
时 / 時	shí	time	4.1
诉 / 訴	sù	tell; relate	8.1
条 / 條	tiáo	M (for long objects)	9.1
听 / 聽	tīng	listen	4.1
位	wèi	M (polite)	6.1
我	wǒ	I; me	1.1
希	xī	hope	8.2
言 (讠)	yán	word	Rad
医 / 醫	yī	doctor; medicine	2.2
员 / 員	yuán	personnel	9.1
园 / 園	yuán	garden	10.1
张 / 張	zhāng	M; (a surname)	2.1
找	zhǎo	look for; seek	4.2
这 / 這	zhè(i)	this	2.1
助	zhù	assist	7.1
走	zǒu	walk	Rad, 11.1
足	zú	foot	Rad
坐	zuò	sit	5.1
作	zuò	work; do	5.1

8

爸	bà	dad	2.1
杯	bēi	cup; glass	5.1
衬 / 襯	chèn	lining	9.1
到	dào	arrive	6.1
的	de	P	2.1
法	fǎ	method; way	7.1
服	fú	clothing	9.1
国 / 國	guó	country	1.2
和	hé/huo	and/*warm	2.2
话 / 話	huà	speech	6.1
货 / 貨	huò	merchandise	9.1
或	huò	or	11.1
金 (钅)	jīn	(a surname); gold	Rad
经 / 經	jīng	pass through	8.1

练 / 練	liàn	practice; drill	6.2
录 / 錄	lù	record	7.2
念 / 唸	niàn	read	7.2
绍 / 紹	shào	carry on	5.1
衫	shān	shirt	9.1
始	shǐ	begin	7.2
事	shì	matter; affair	3.2
视 / 視	shì	view	4.1
试 / 試	shì	try	6.1
所 (所)	suǒ	*so; place	4.1
图 / 圖	tú	drawing	5.2
现 / 現	xiàn	present	3.2
线 / 線	xiàn	line	11.1
姓	xìng	surname	1.1
学 / 學	xué	study	1.2
夜	yè	night	7.2
宜	yí	suitable	9.1
易	yì	easy	7.1
英 / 英	yīng	*England	2.2
雨	yǔ	rain	Rad, 10.1
周 / 週	zhōu	week	4.1
隹	zhuī	short-tailed bird	Rad

9

帮 / 幫	bāng	help	6.2
便	biàn	convenient	6.1
茶 / 茶	chá	tea	5.1
除 / 除	chú	except	8.2
穿	chuān	wear	9.1
春	chūn	spring	10.2
点 / 點	diǎn	dot; o'clock	3.1
封	fēng	M (for letters)	8.2
复 / 復	fù	duplicate	7.1
给 / 給	gěi	give	5.1
贵 / 貴	guì	honorable	1.1

孩	hái	child	2.1
很	hěn	very	3.2
候	hòu	wait	4.1
觉／覺	jiào	feel; reckon	4.2
觉／覺	jué	feel; reckon	4.2
看	kàn	see; look	4.1
客	kè	guest	4.1
亮／亮	liàng	bright	5.1
律	lù	law; rule	2.2
美	měi	beautiful	1.2
哪／哪	nǎ / něi	which	5.1
便	pián	*inexpensive	9.1
前	qián	front; before	8.1
秋	qiū	autumn; fall	10.2
食(饣)	shí	to eat	Rad
是	shì	be	1.2
室	shì	room	6.1
适／適	shì	suit; fit	9.2
帅	shuài	handsome	7.2
说／説	shuō	speak	6.2
思	sī	think	4.2
送／送	sòng	deliver	11.1
虽／雖	suī	though; while	9.2
洗	xǐ	wash	8.1
信	xìn	letter	8.2
星	xīng	star	3.1
要	yào	want	5.1
音	yīn	sound; music	4.1
语／語	yǔ	language	7.1
怎	zěn	*how	3.1
钟／鐘	zhōng	clock	3.1
祝	zhù	wish	8.2
昨	zuó	yesterday	4.1

10

啊／啊	a	P	6.2
笔／筆	bǐ	pen	7.1
都／都	dōu	all; both	2.2
烦／煩	fán	bother	11.1
高	gāo	tall	2.1
哥	gē	older brother	2.2
海	hǎi	sea	10.1
换／換	huàn	change	9.2
家	jiā	family; home	2.2
紧／緊	jǐn	tight	11.2
酒	jiǔ	wine	5.1
课／課	kè	class; lesson	6.1
凉／涼	liáng	cool	10.2
难／難	nán	difficult; hard	7.1
脑／腦	nǎo	brain	8.1
能	néng	be able	8.2
瓶	píng	bottle	5.2
起	qǐ	rise	5.1
钱／錢	qián	money	9.1
请／請	qǐng	please; invite	1.1
热／熱	rè	hot	10.2
容	róng	hold; contain	7.1
谁／誰	shéi	who	2.1
速／速	sù	speed	11.2
铁／鐵	tiě	iron	11.1
夏	xià	summer	10.2
校	xiào	school	5.1
笑	xiào	laugh	8.2
样／樣	yàng	kind	3.1
预／預	yù	prepare	7.1
真(眞)	zhēn	true; real	7.2
租	zū	rent	11.1

	16				17		
餐	cān	meal	8.1	糟	zāo	messy	10.2
糕	gāo	cake	10.2				
澡	zǎo	bath	8.1				

NOTES: